This Book Belongs
to

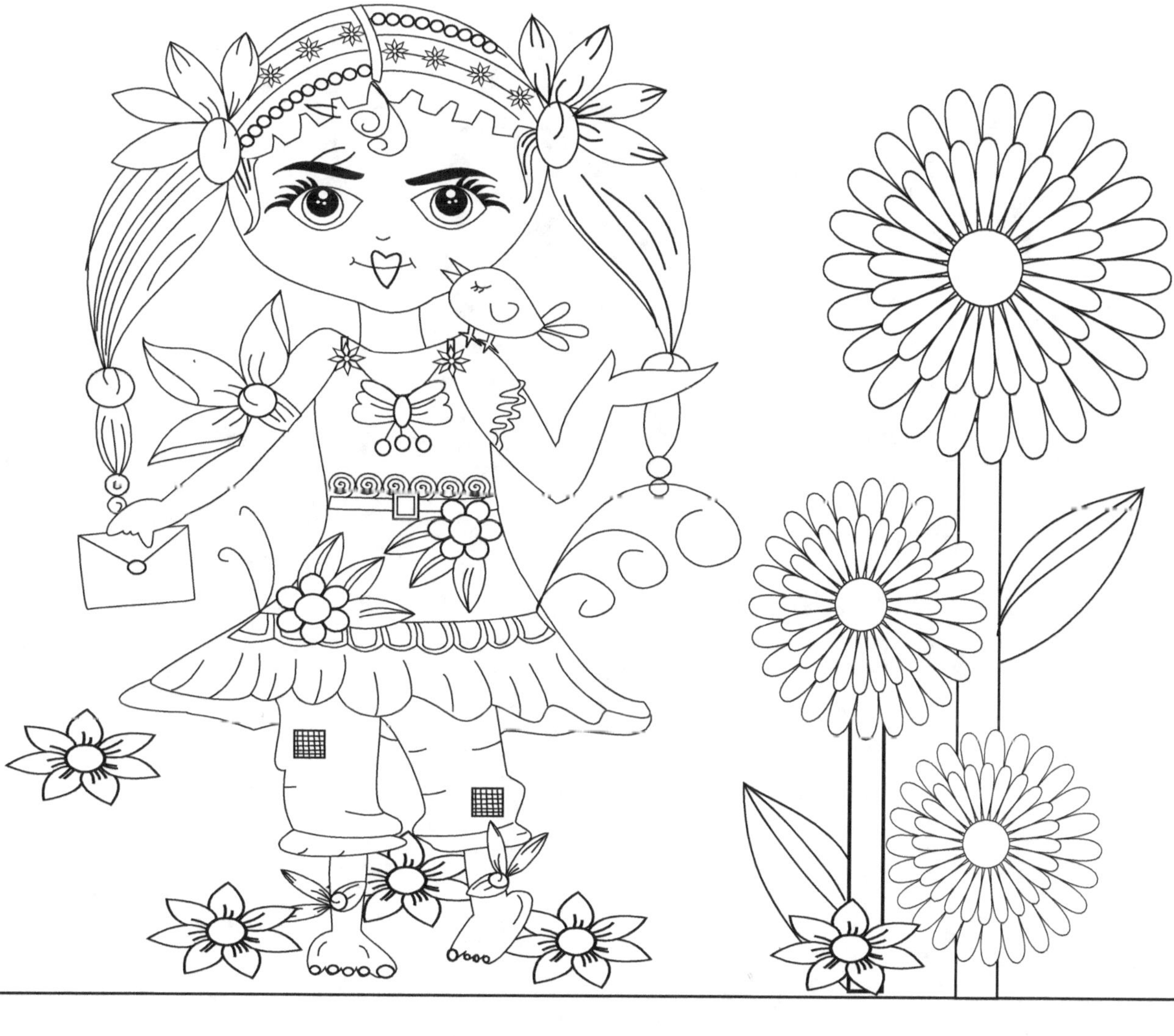

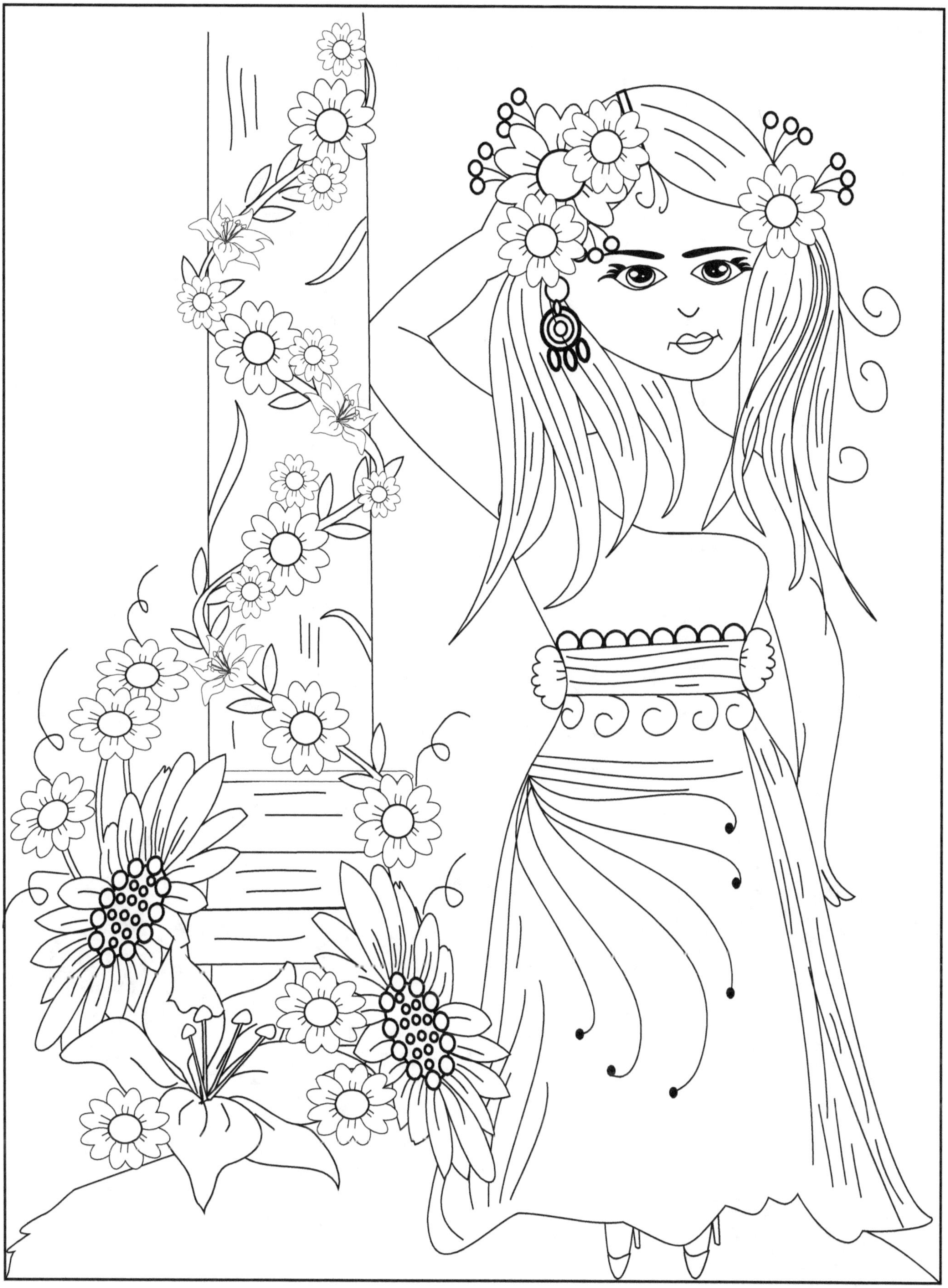

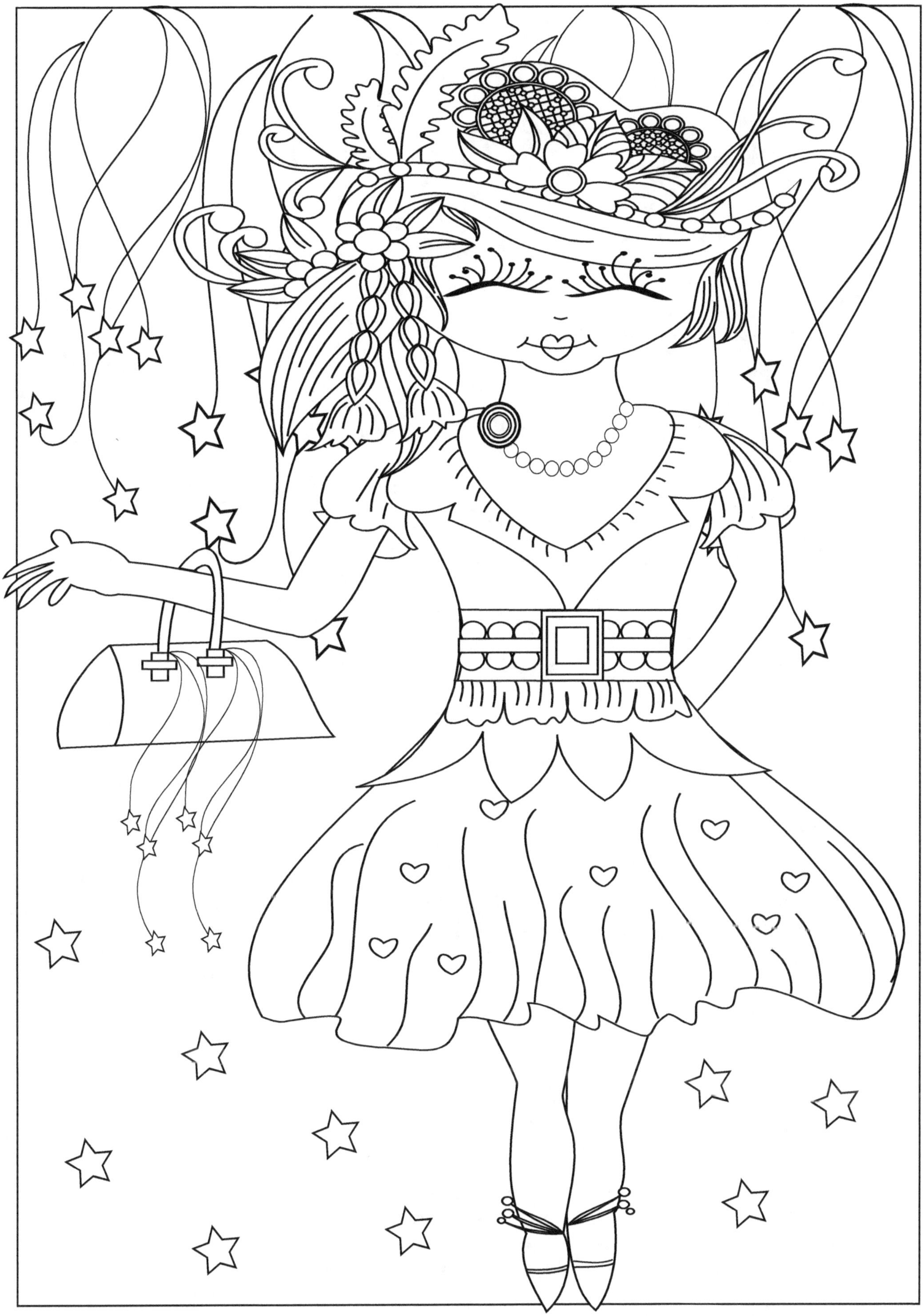

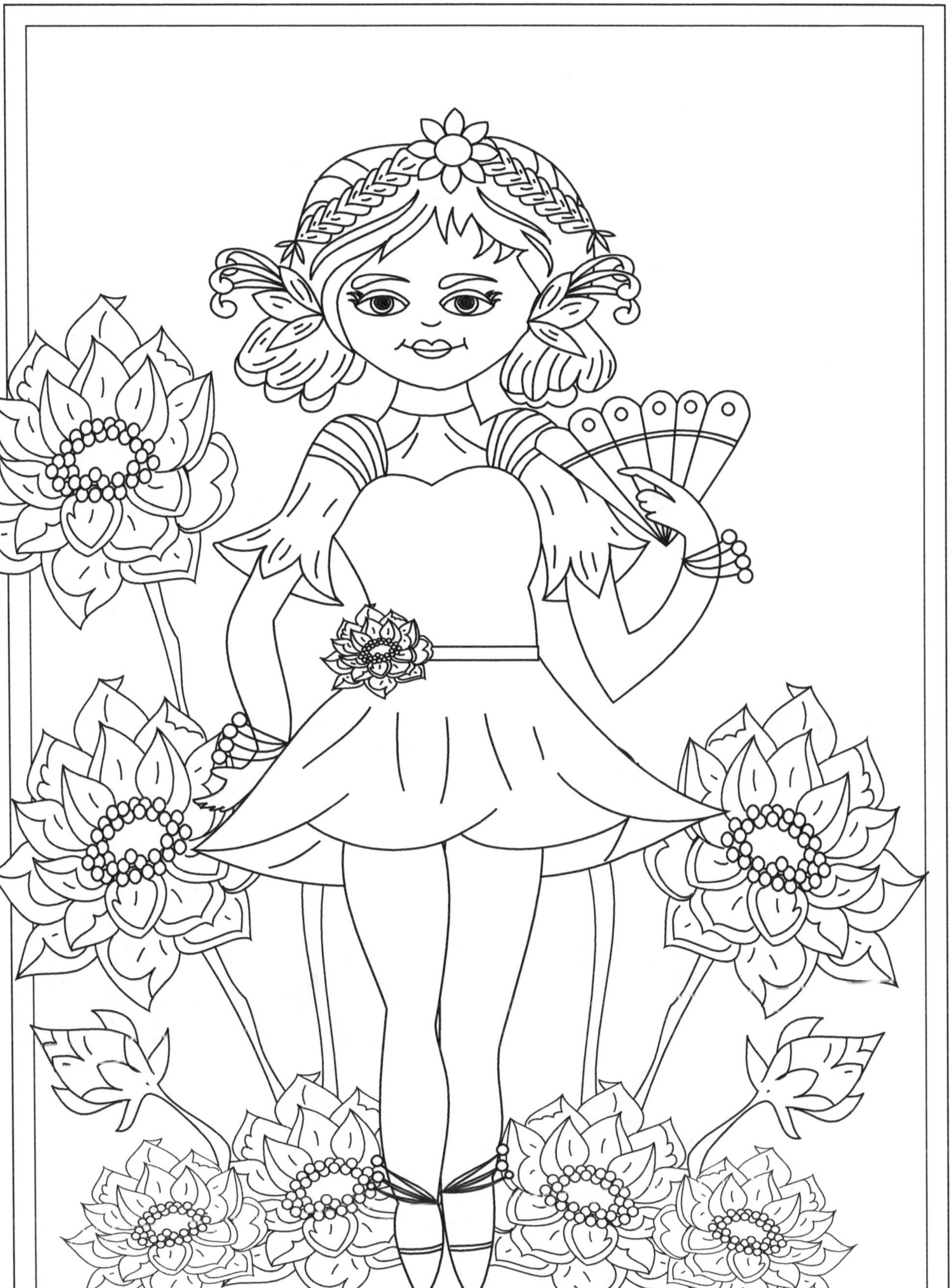

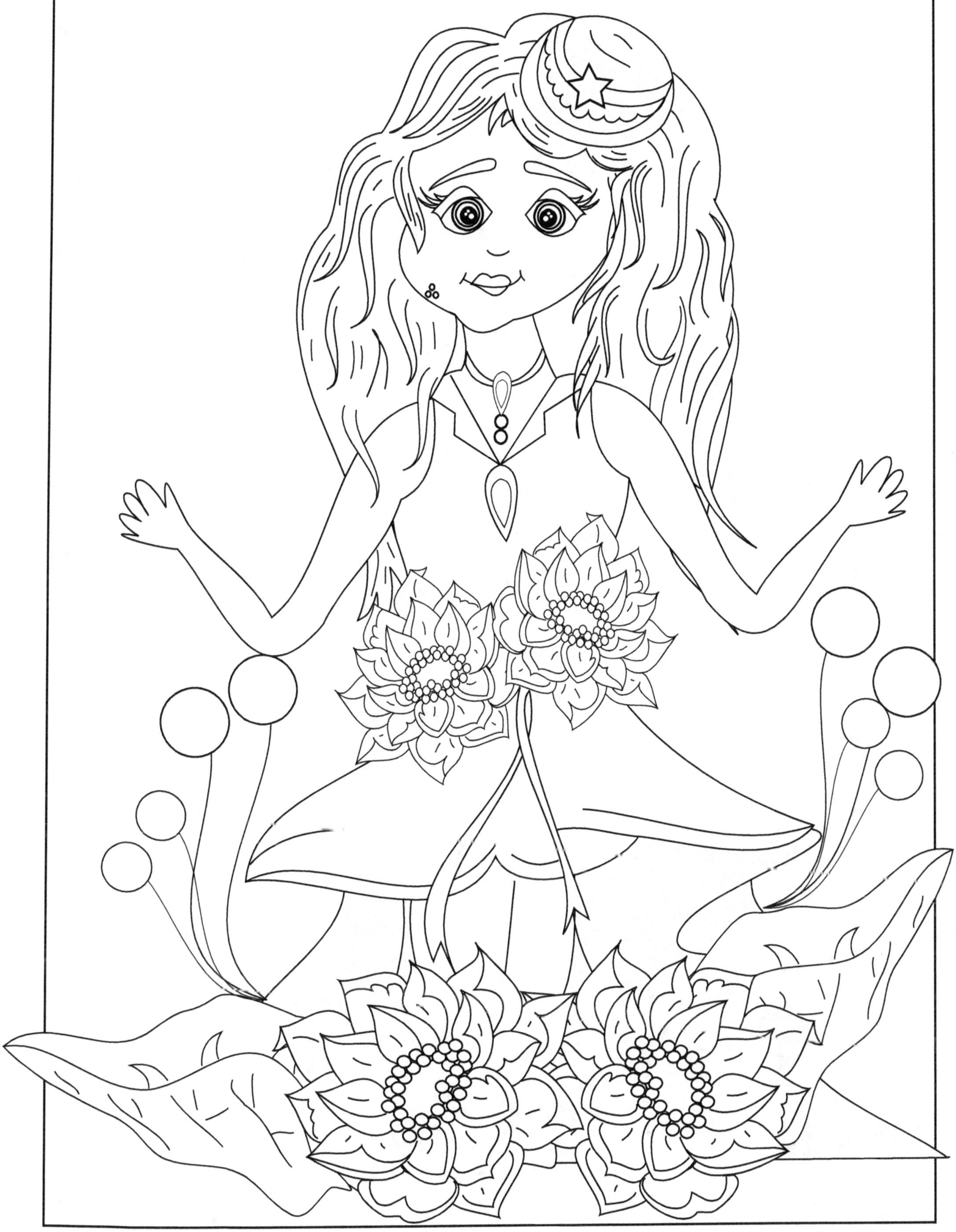

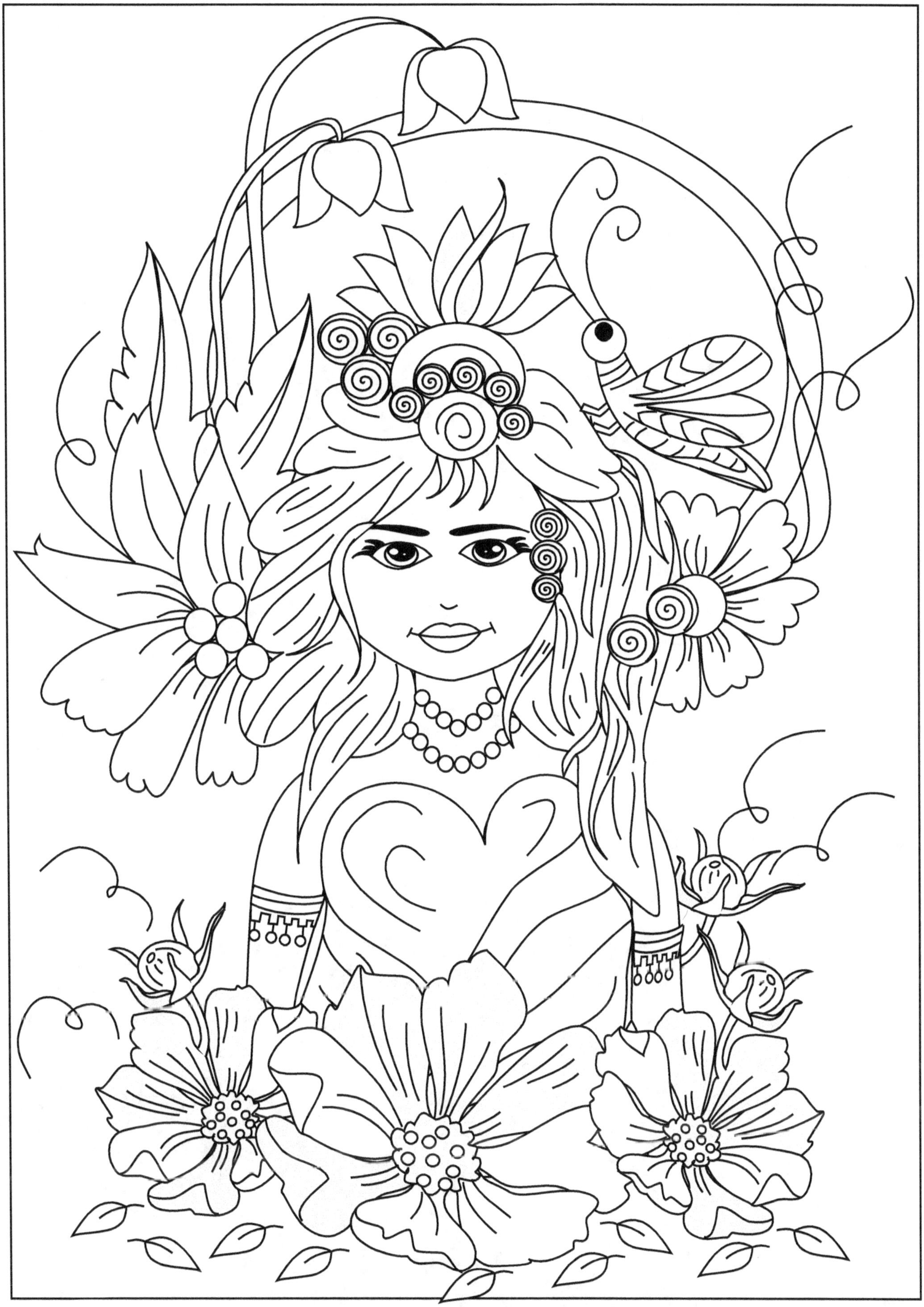

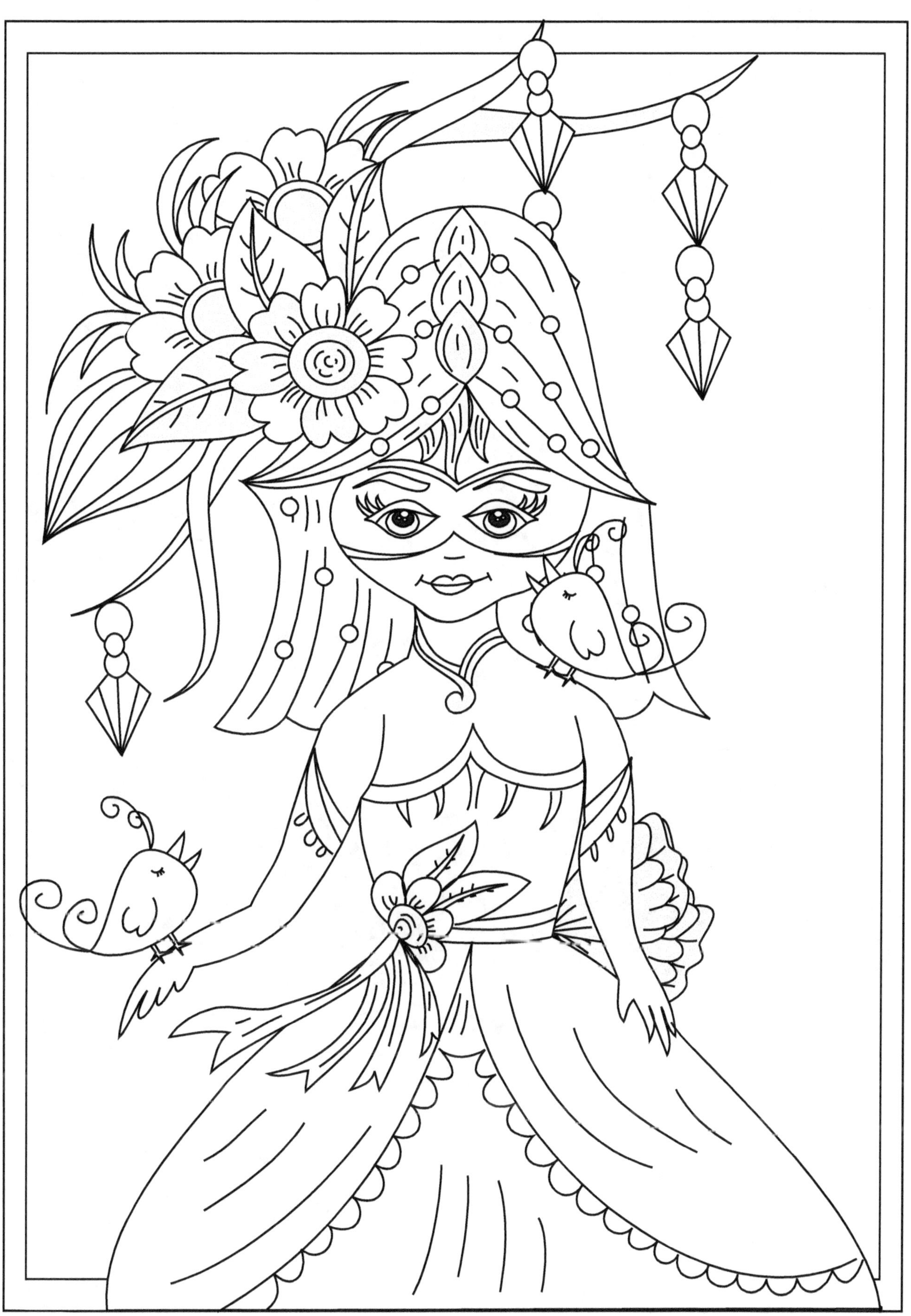

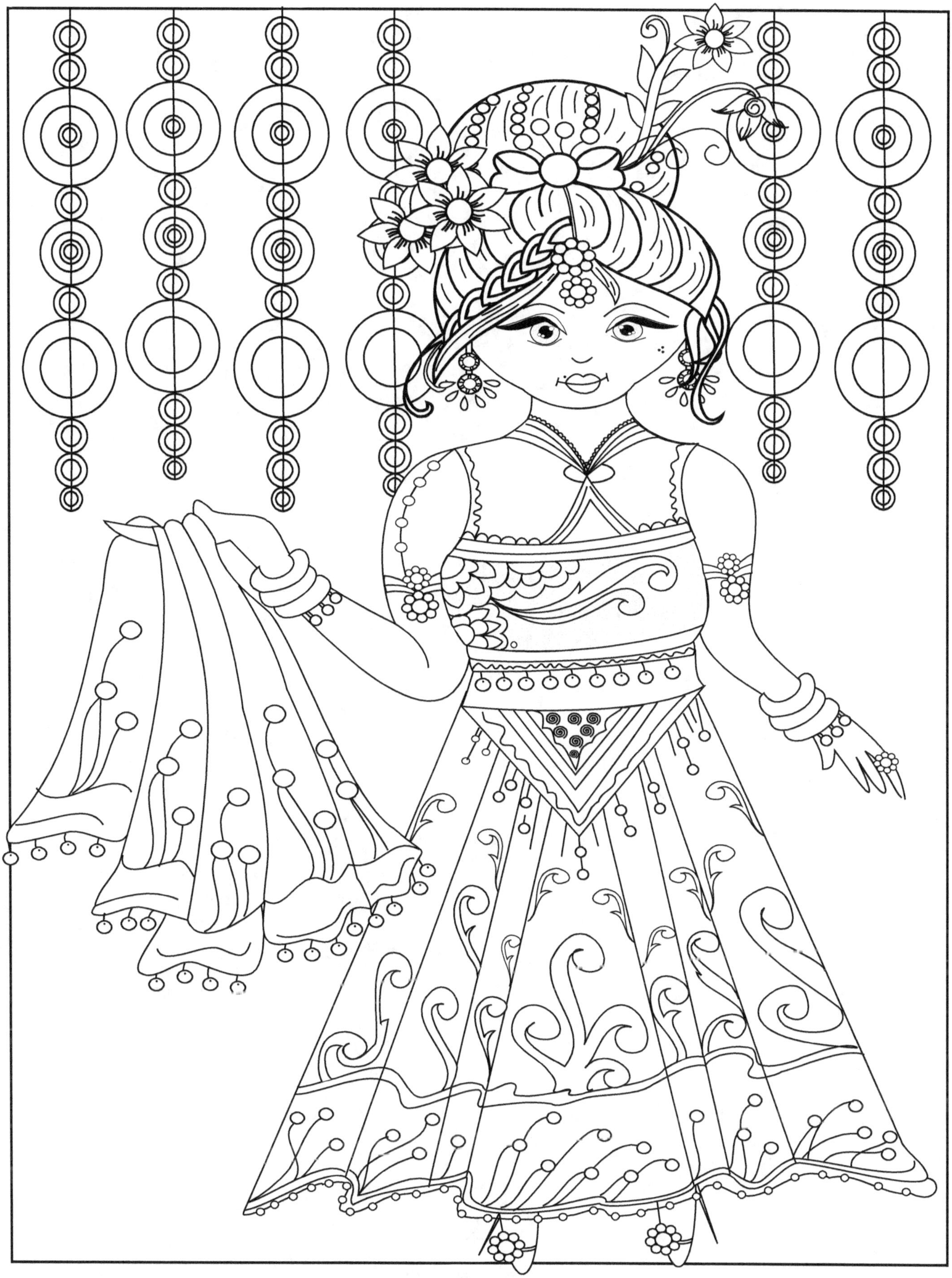

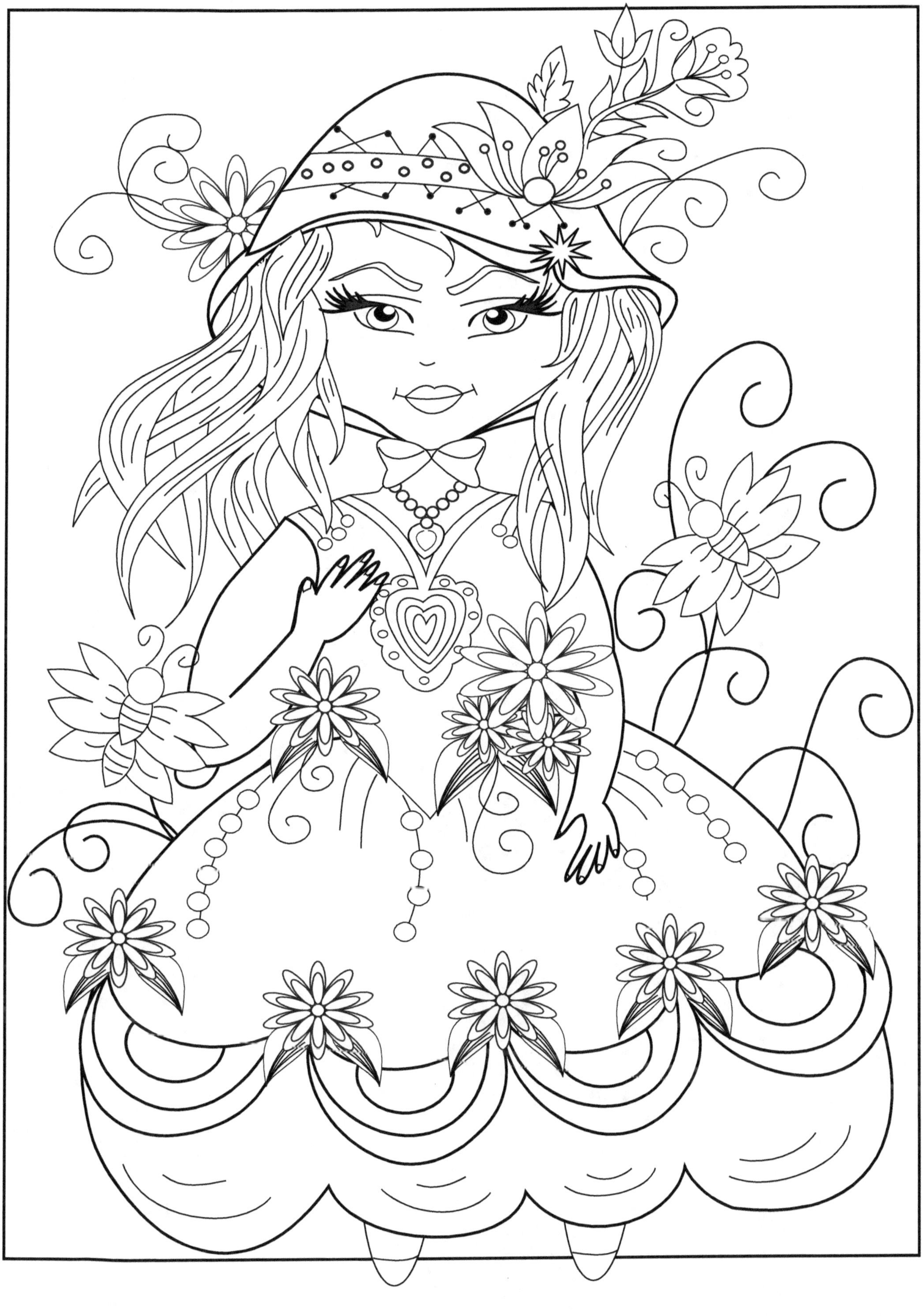

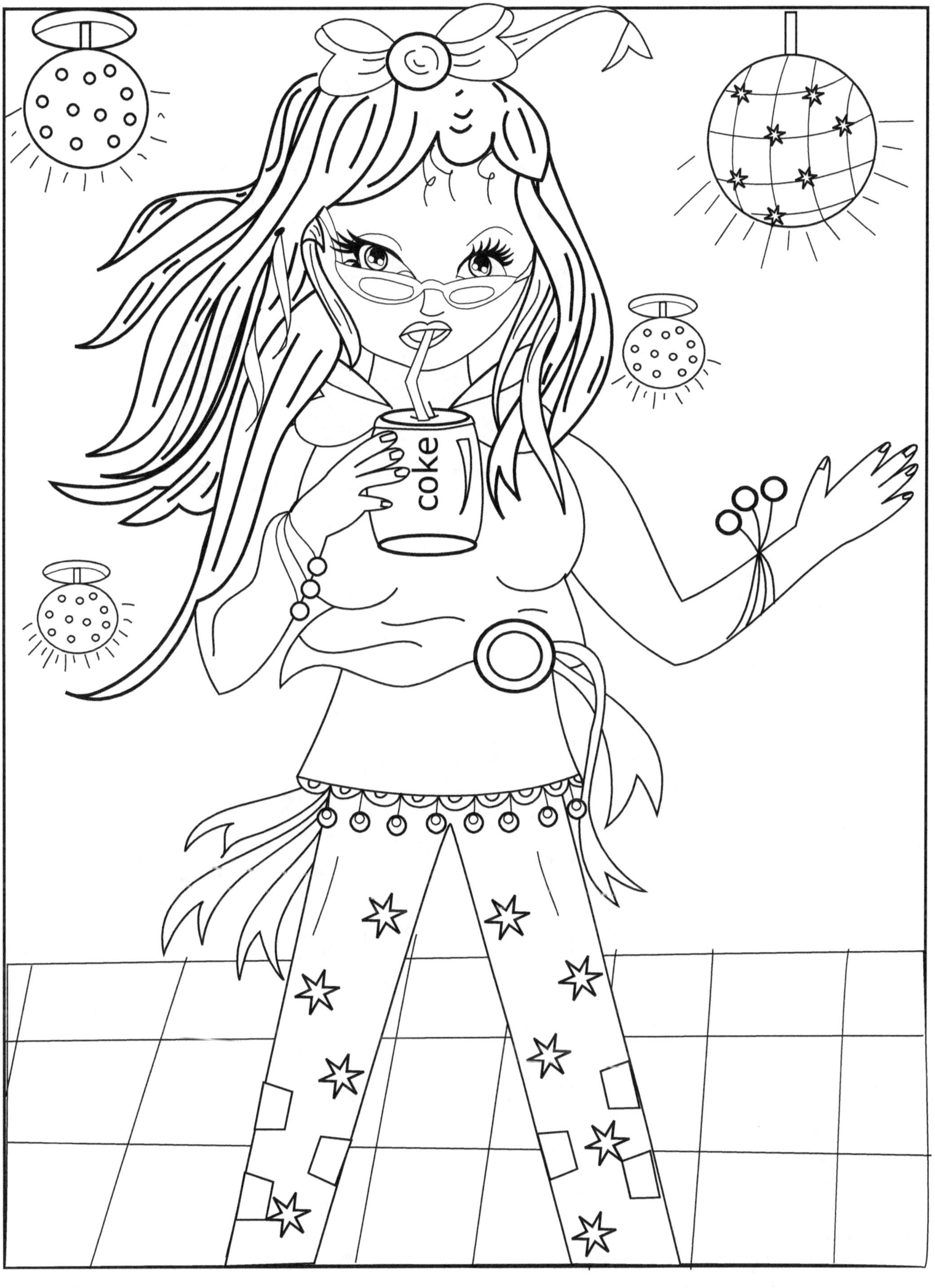
coke

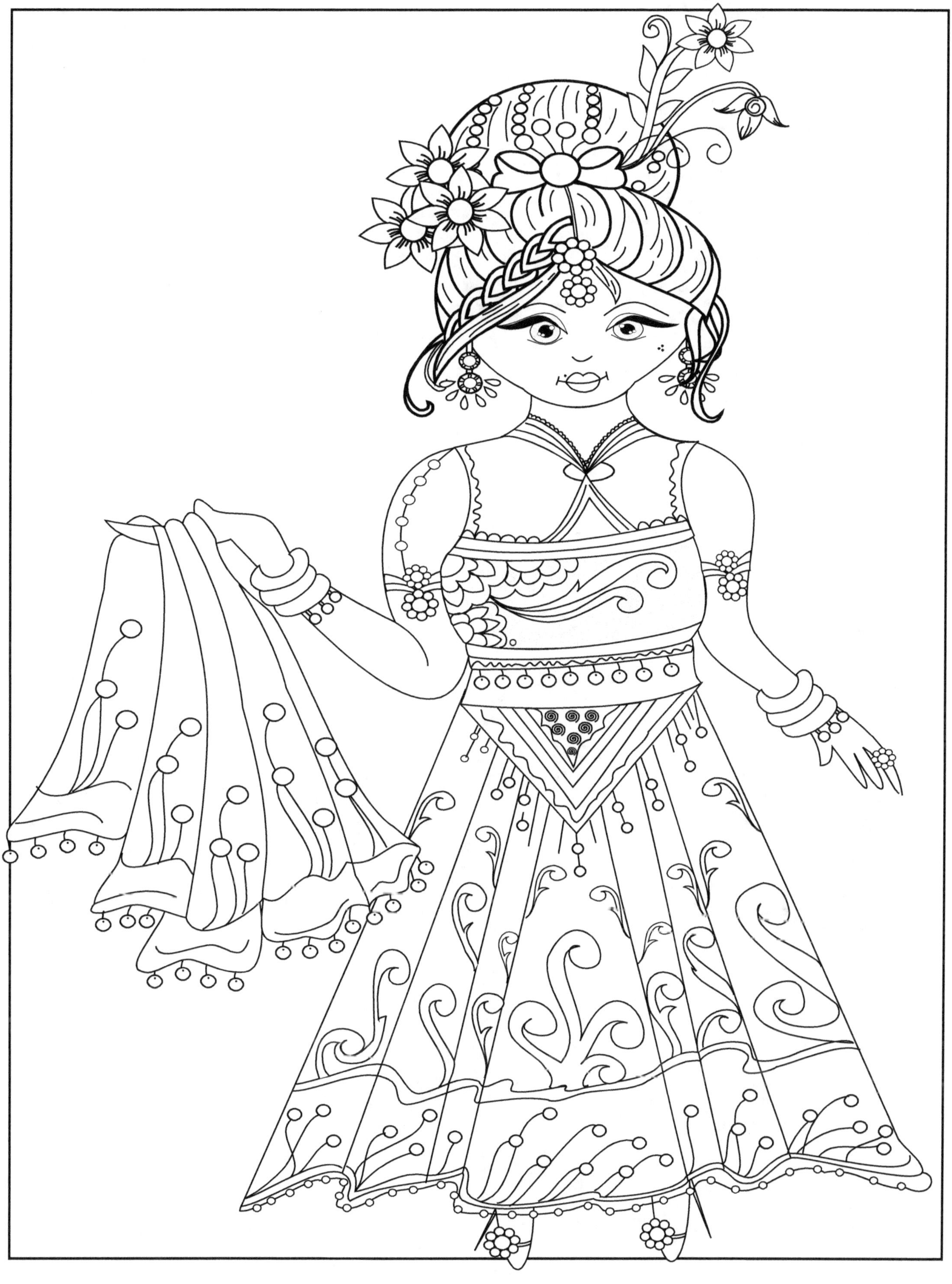

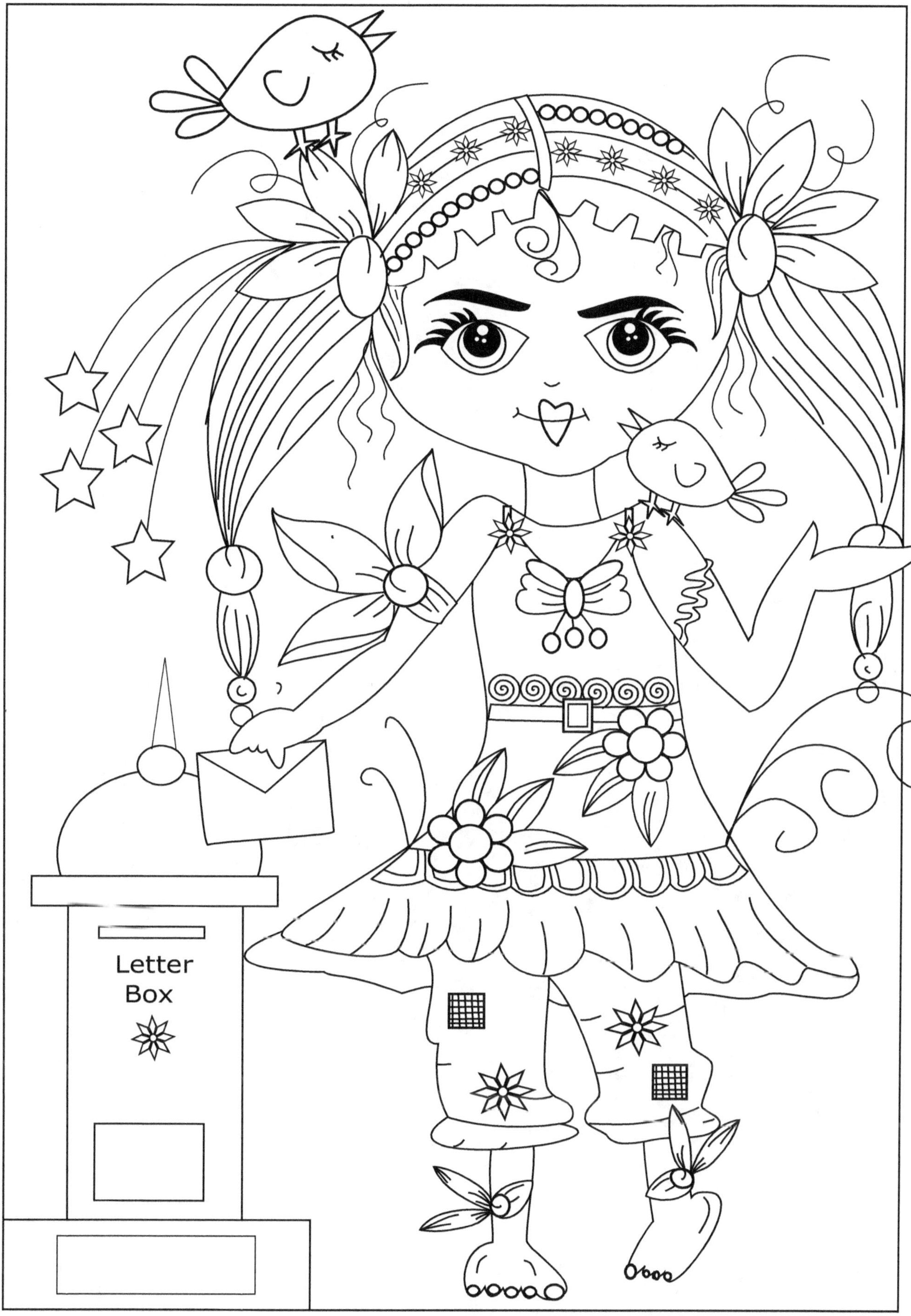
Letter
Box

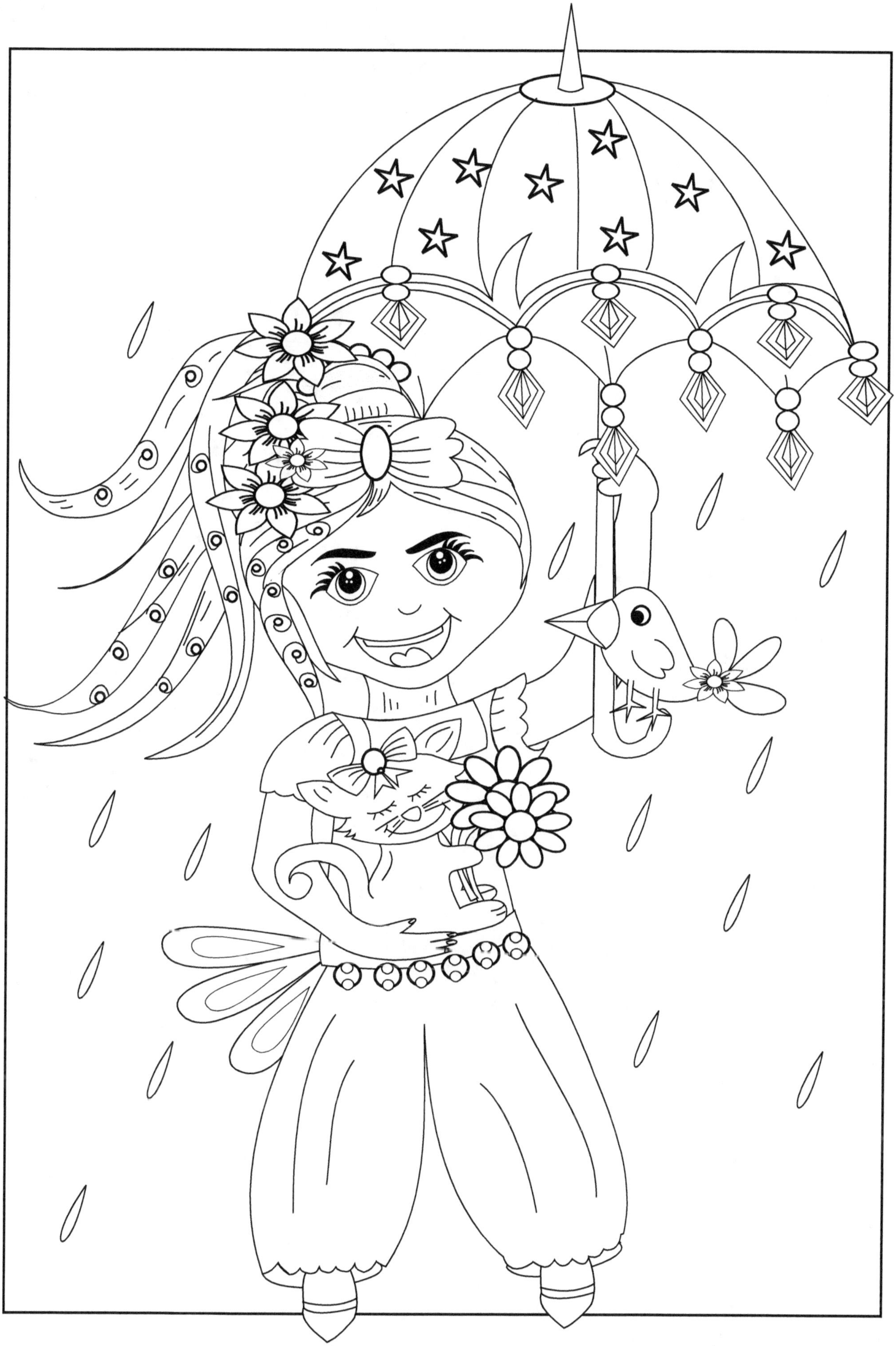

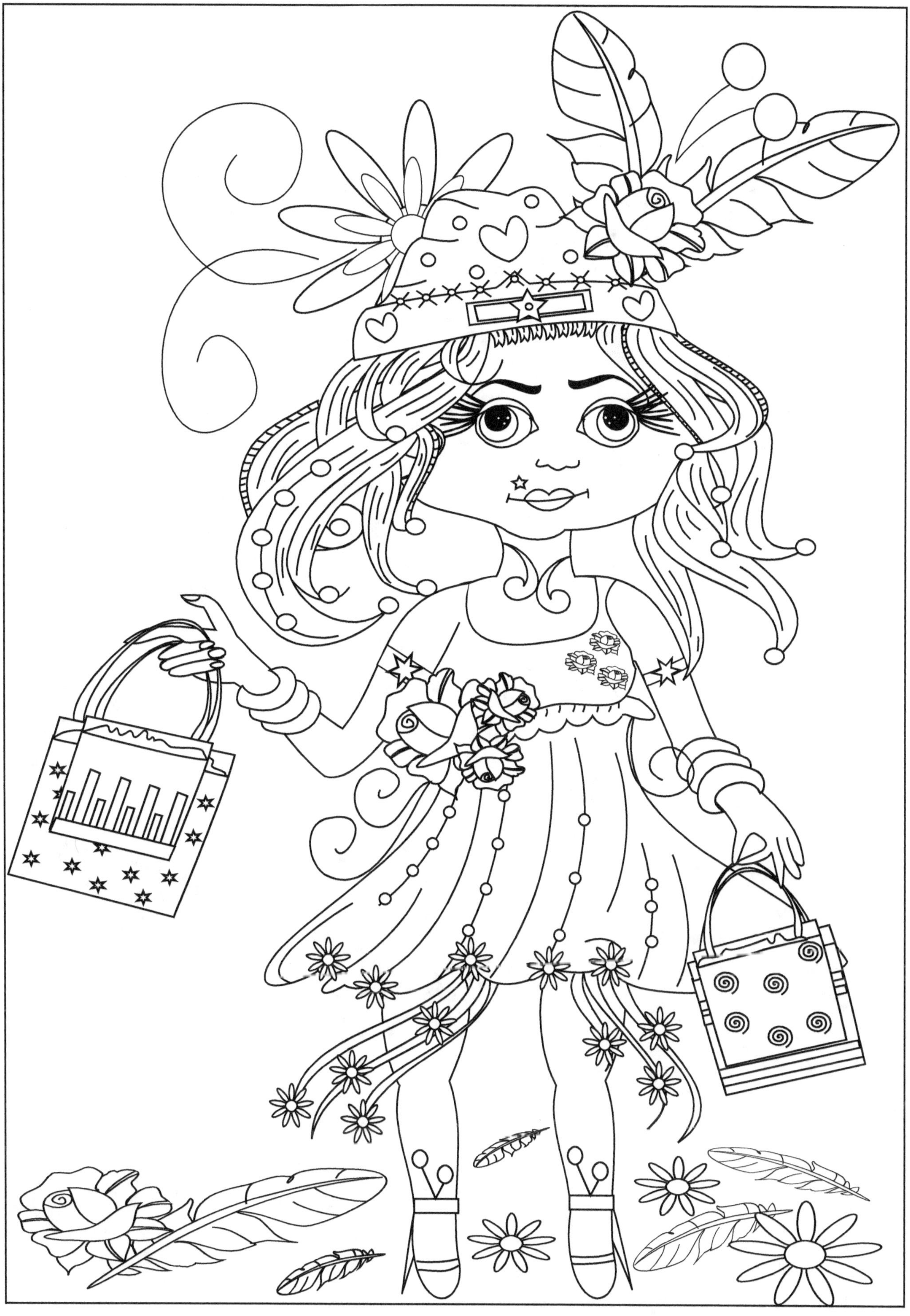

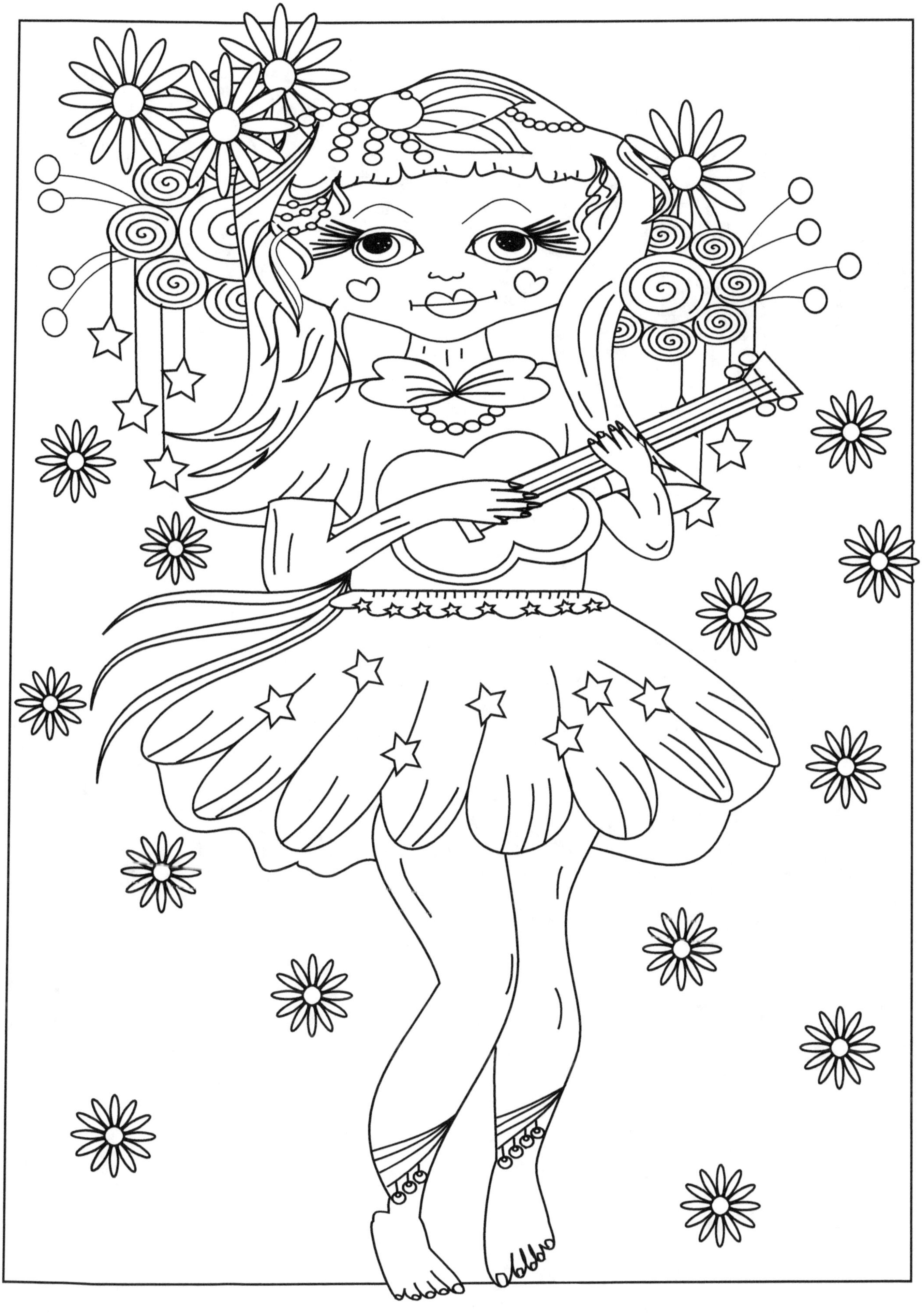

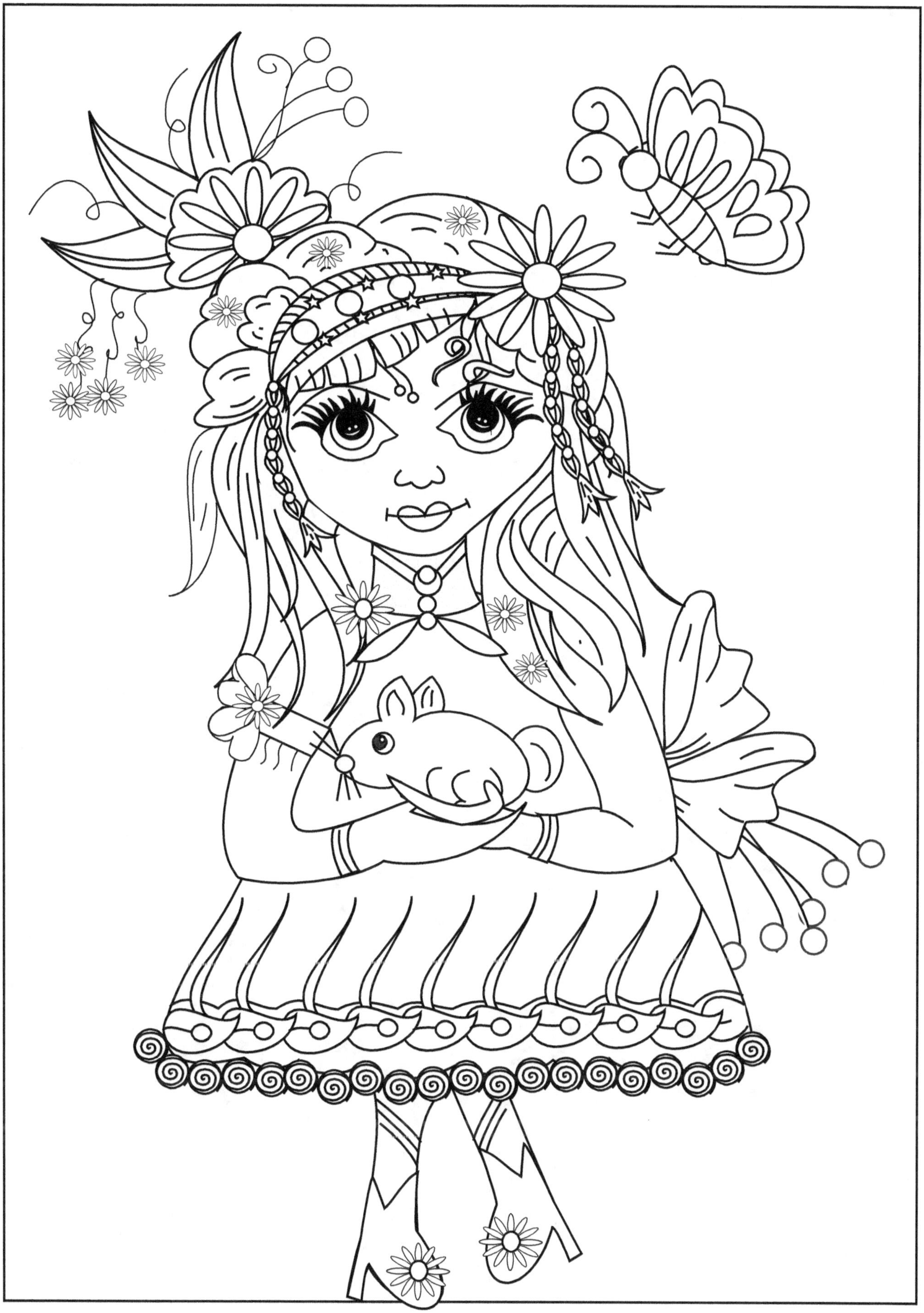

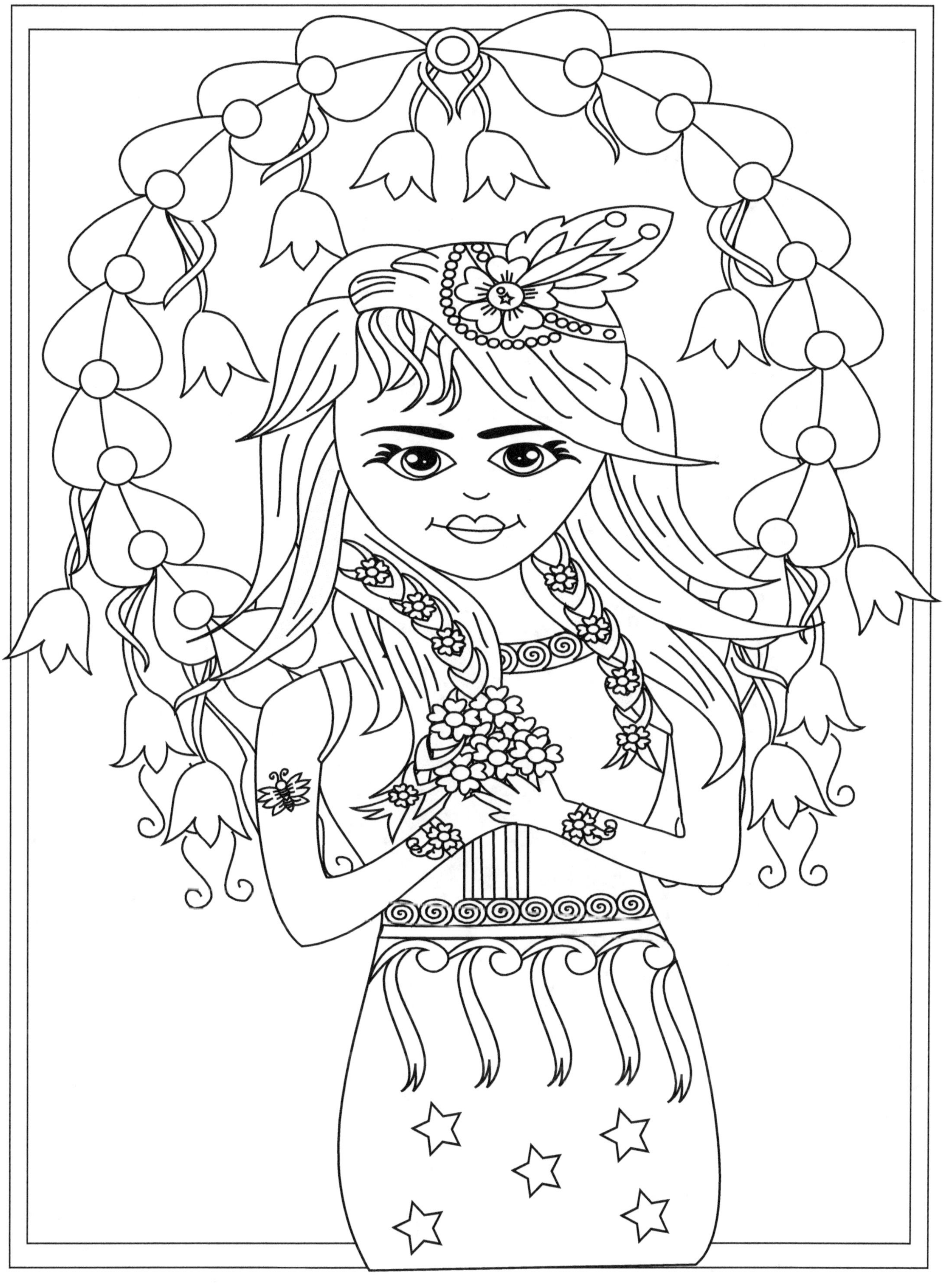

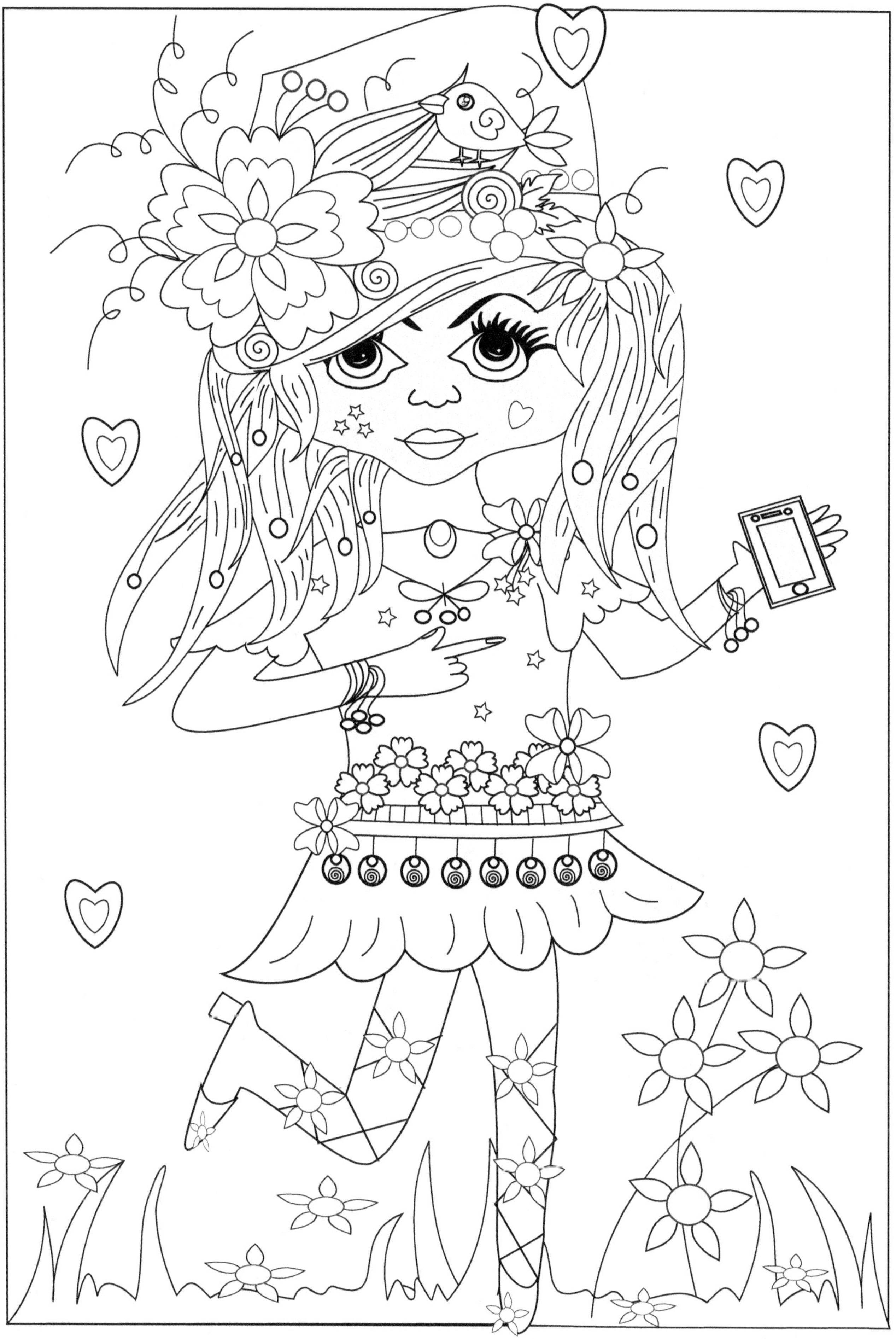

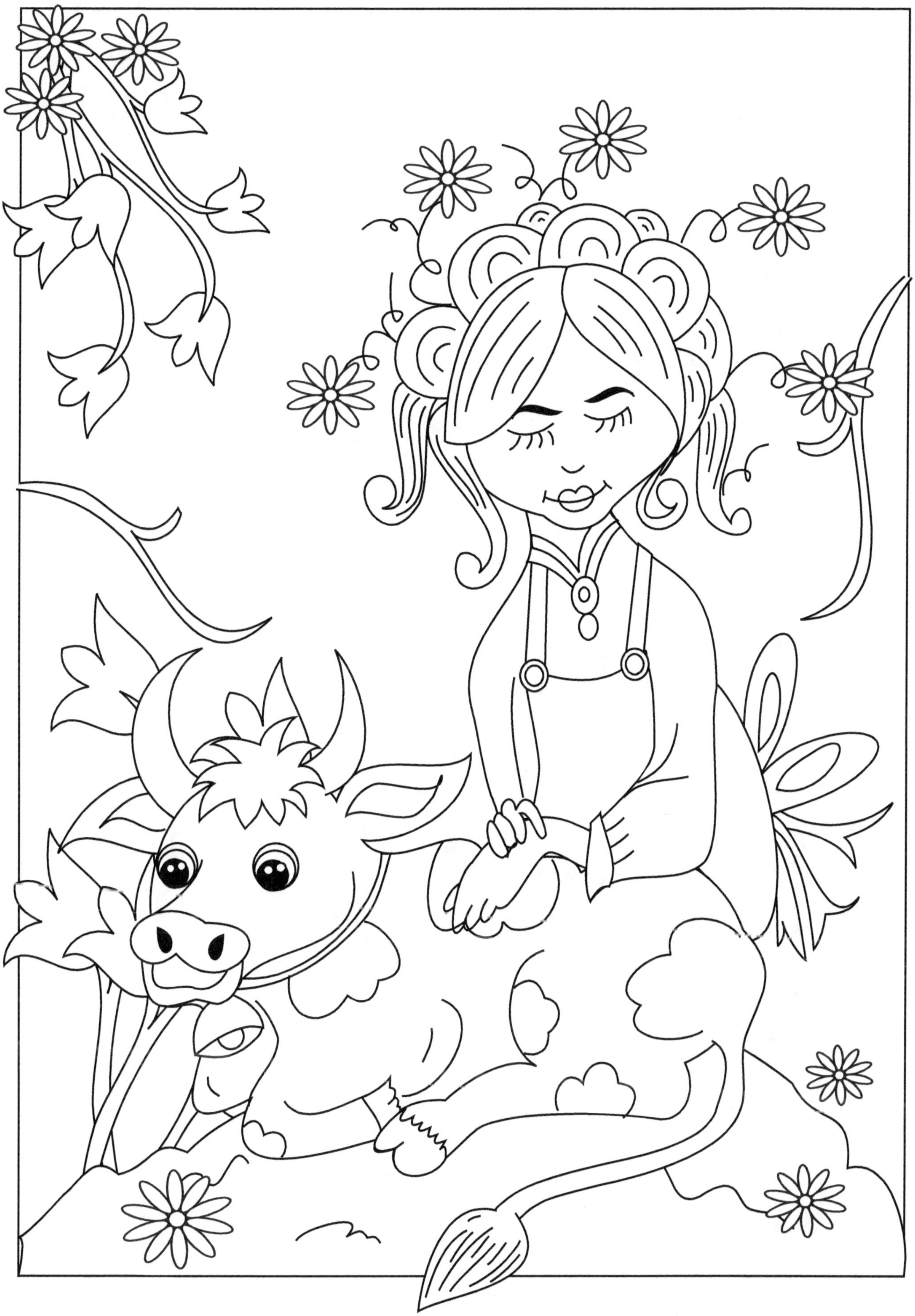

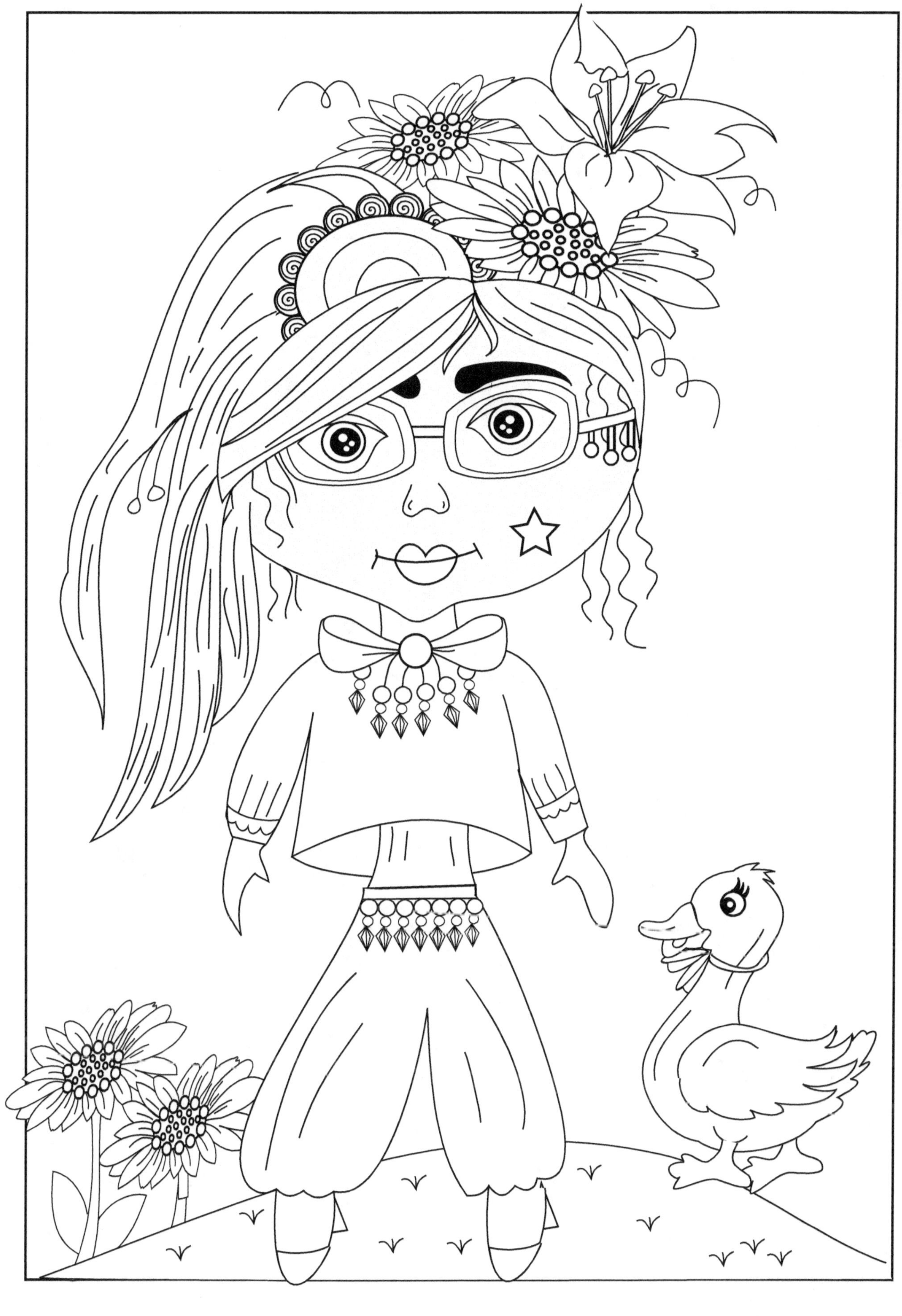

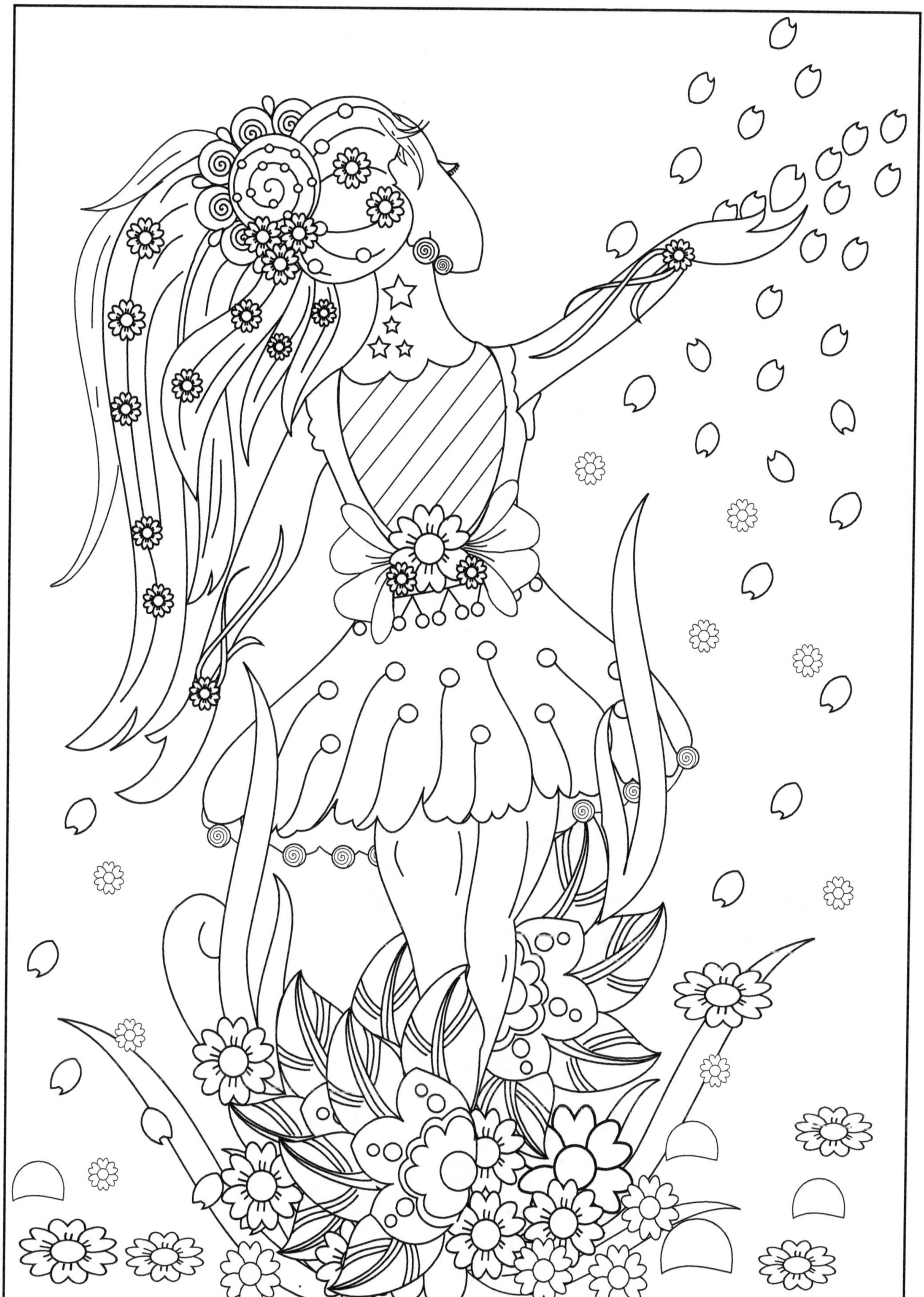

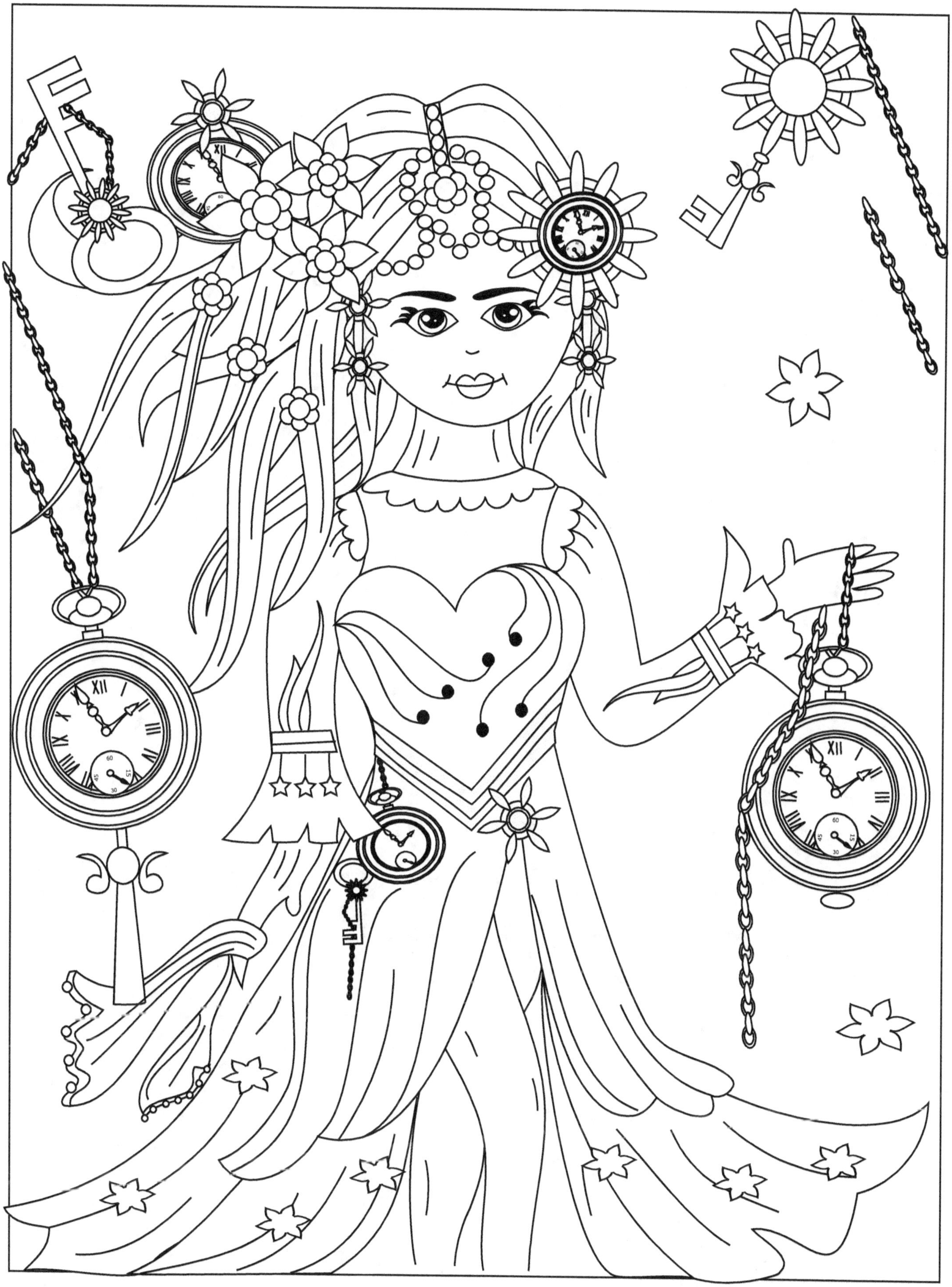

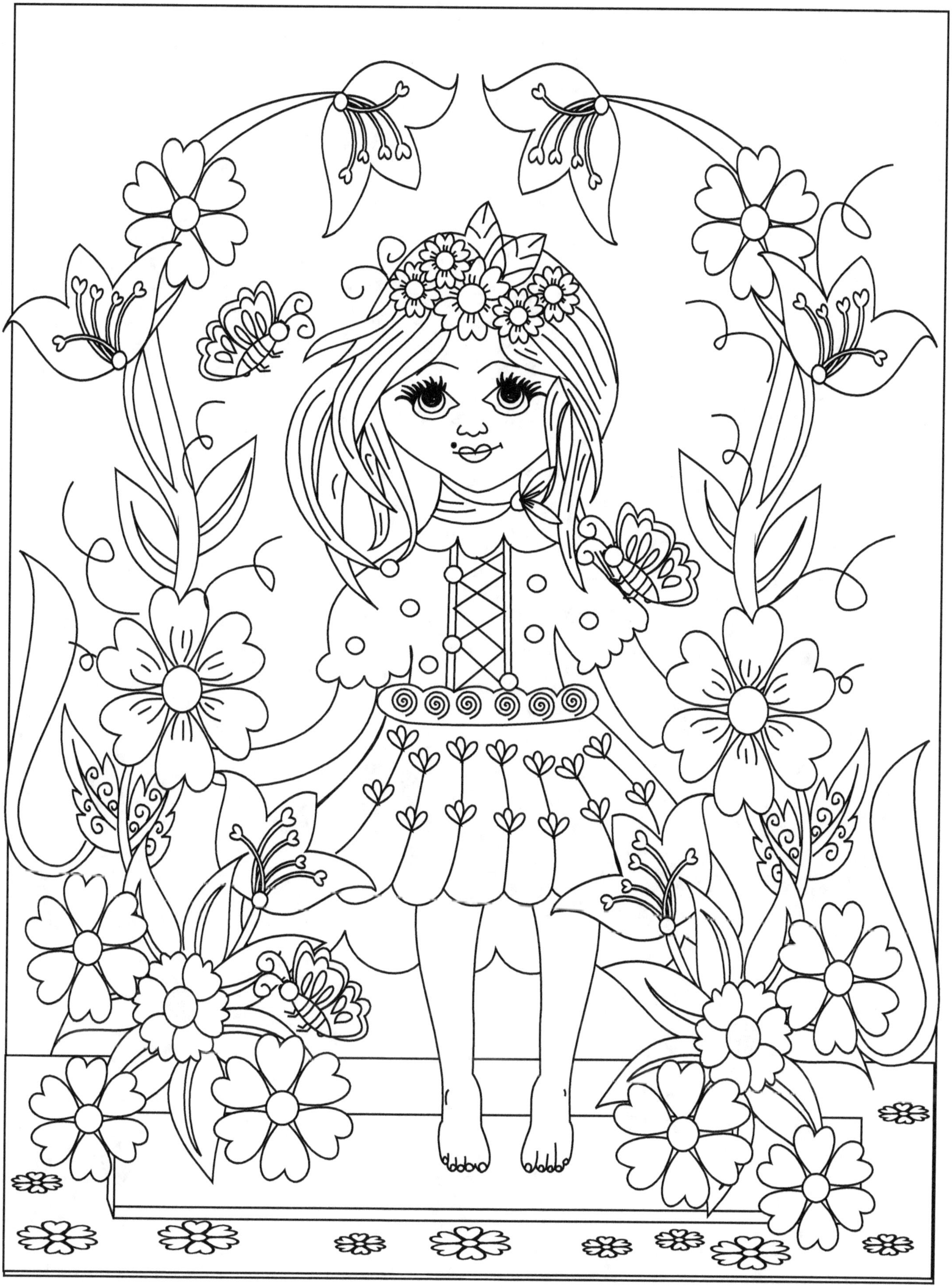

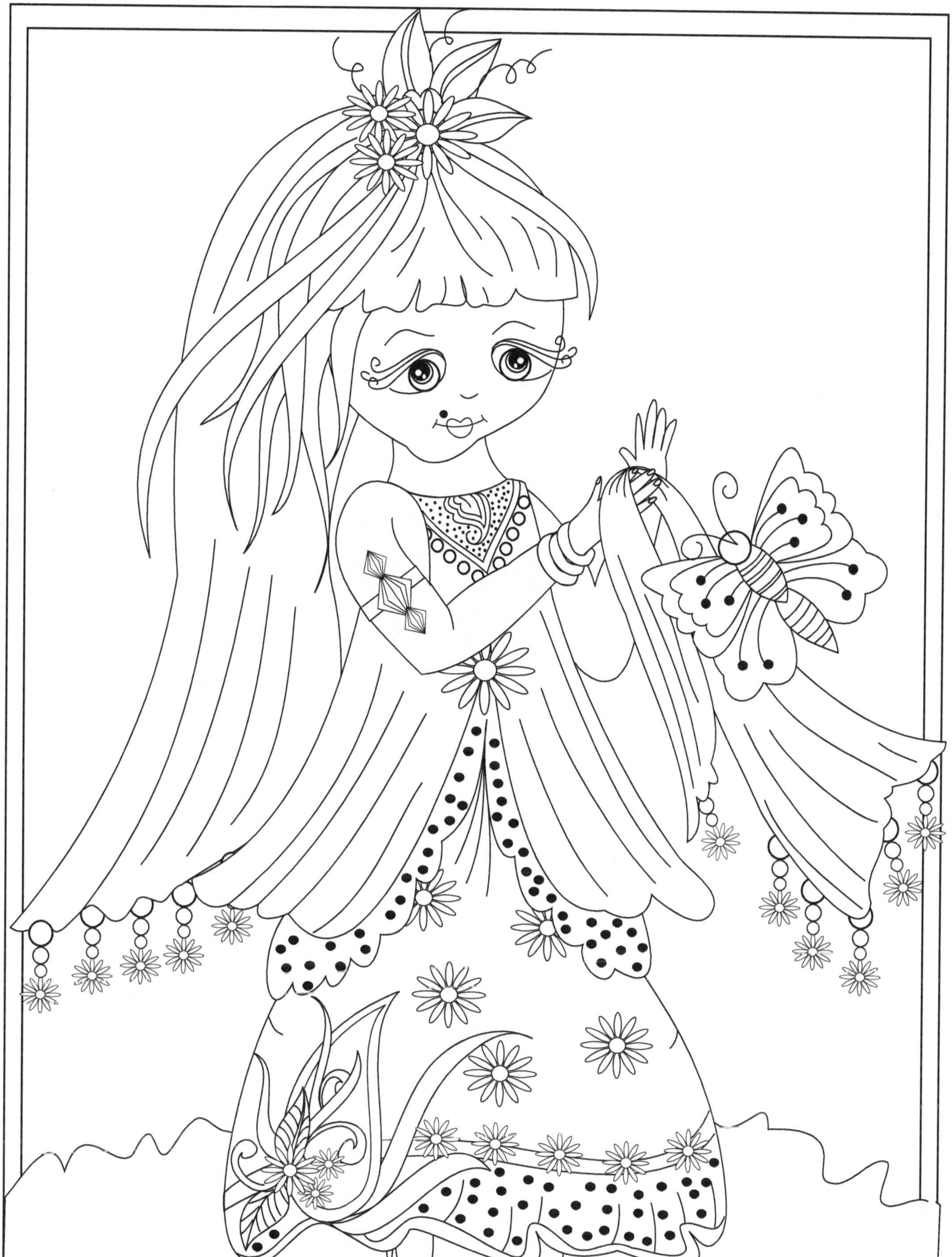

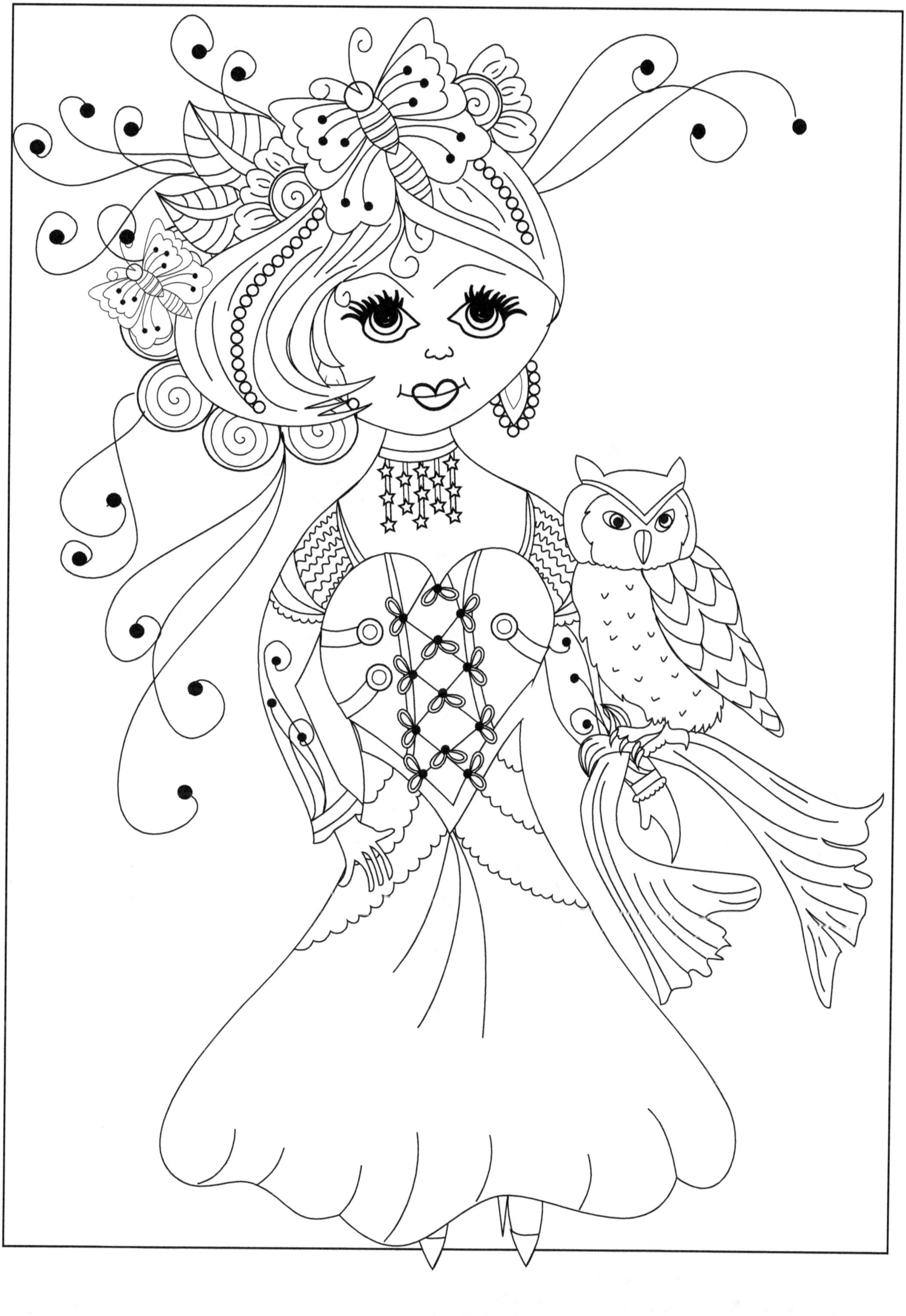

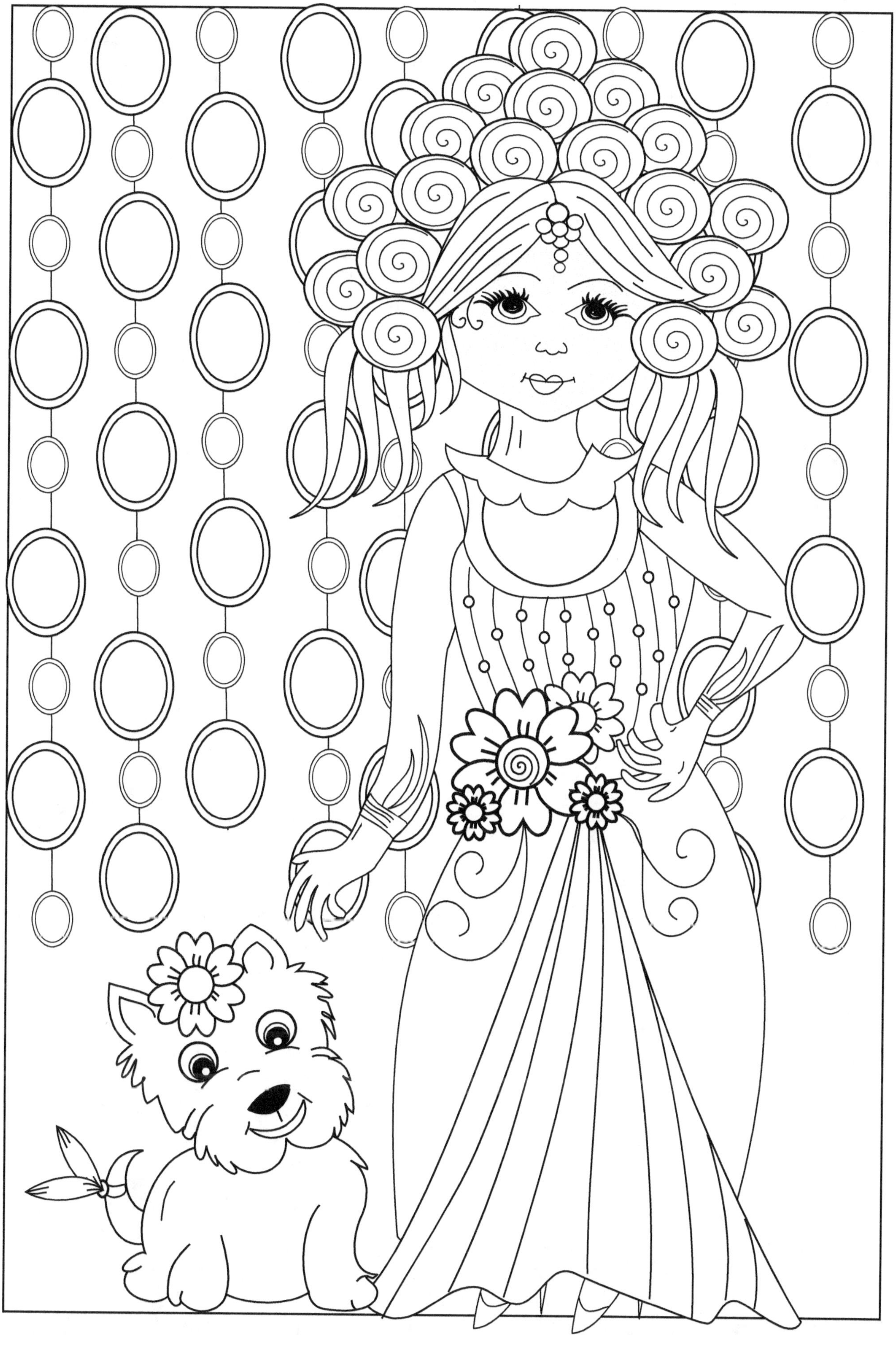

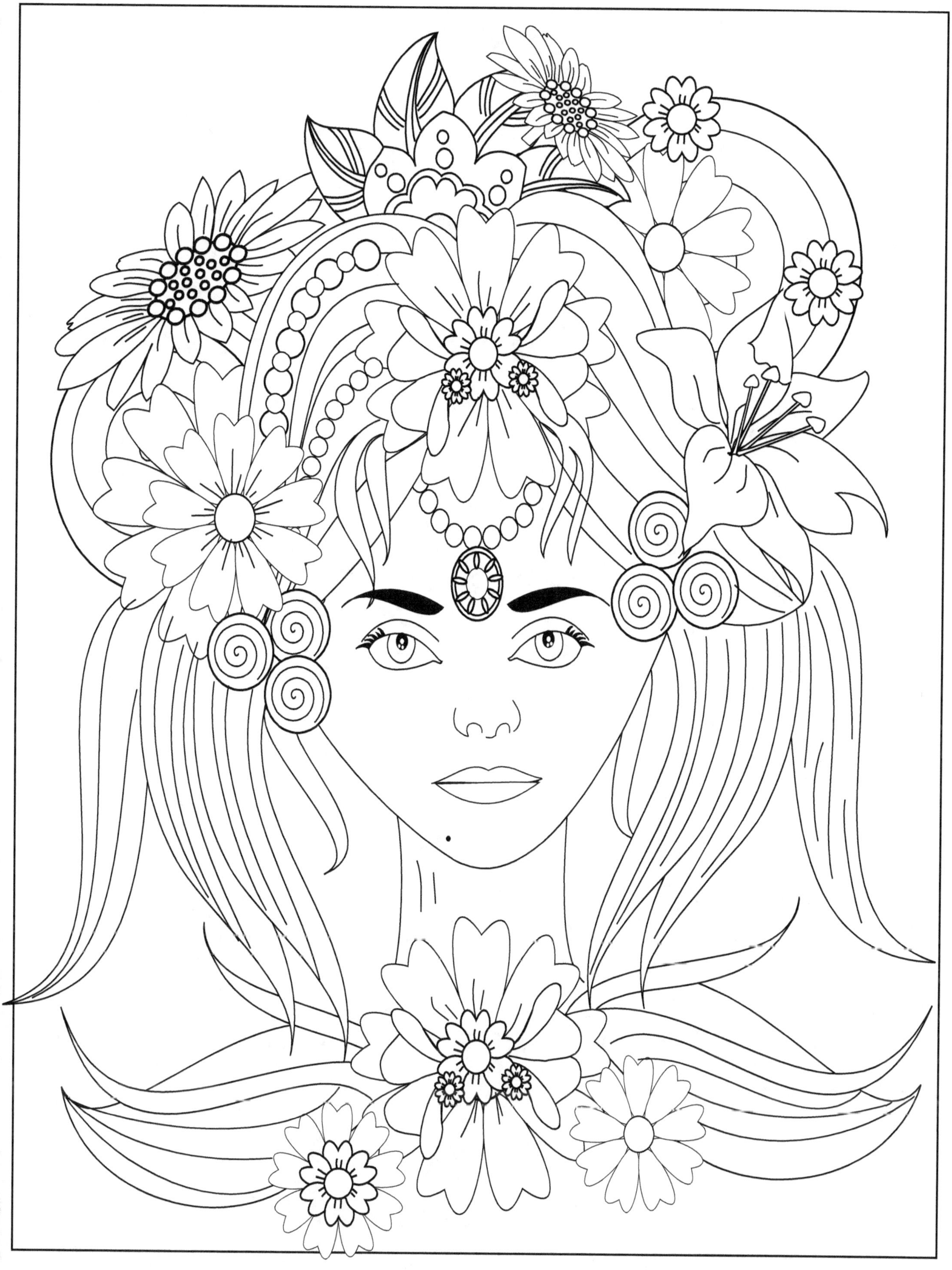

Color test

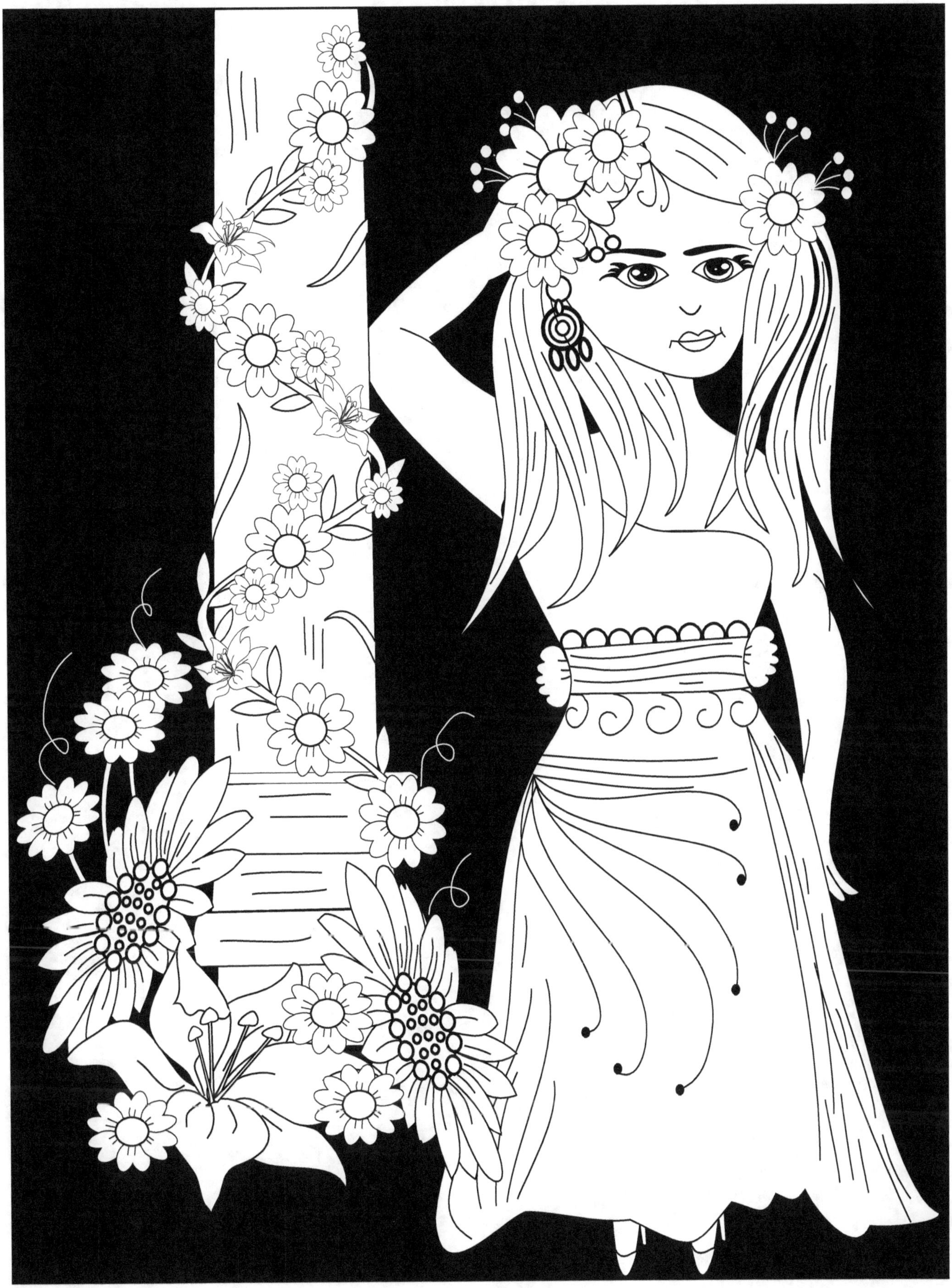

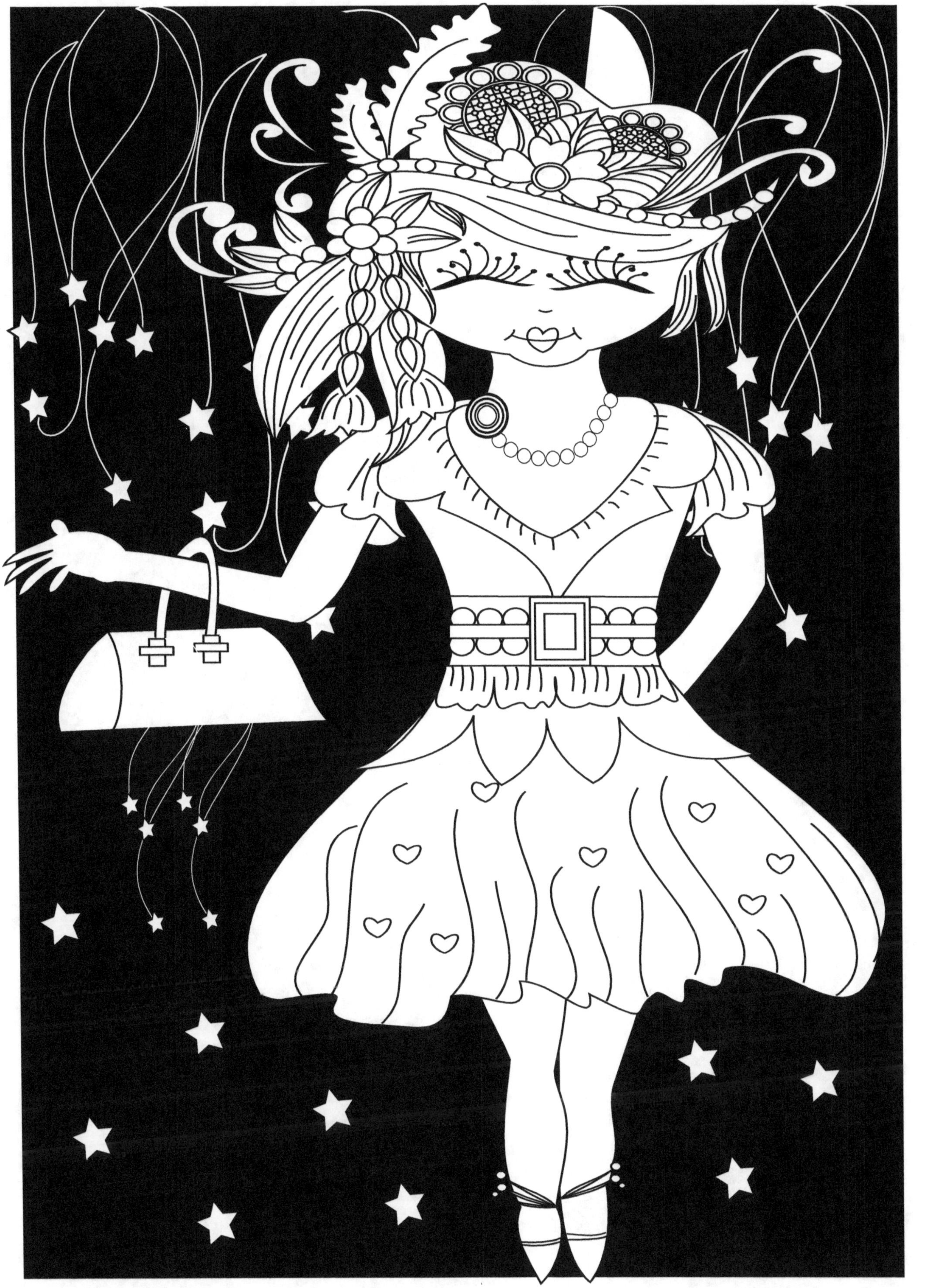

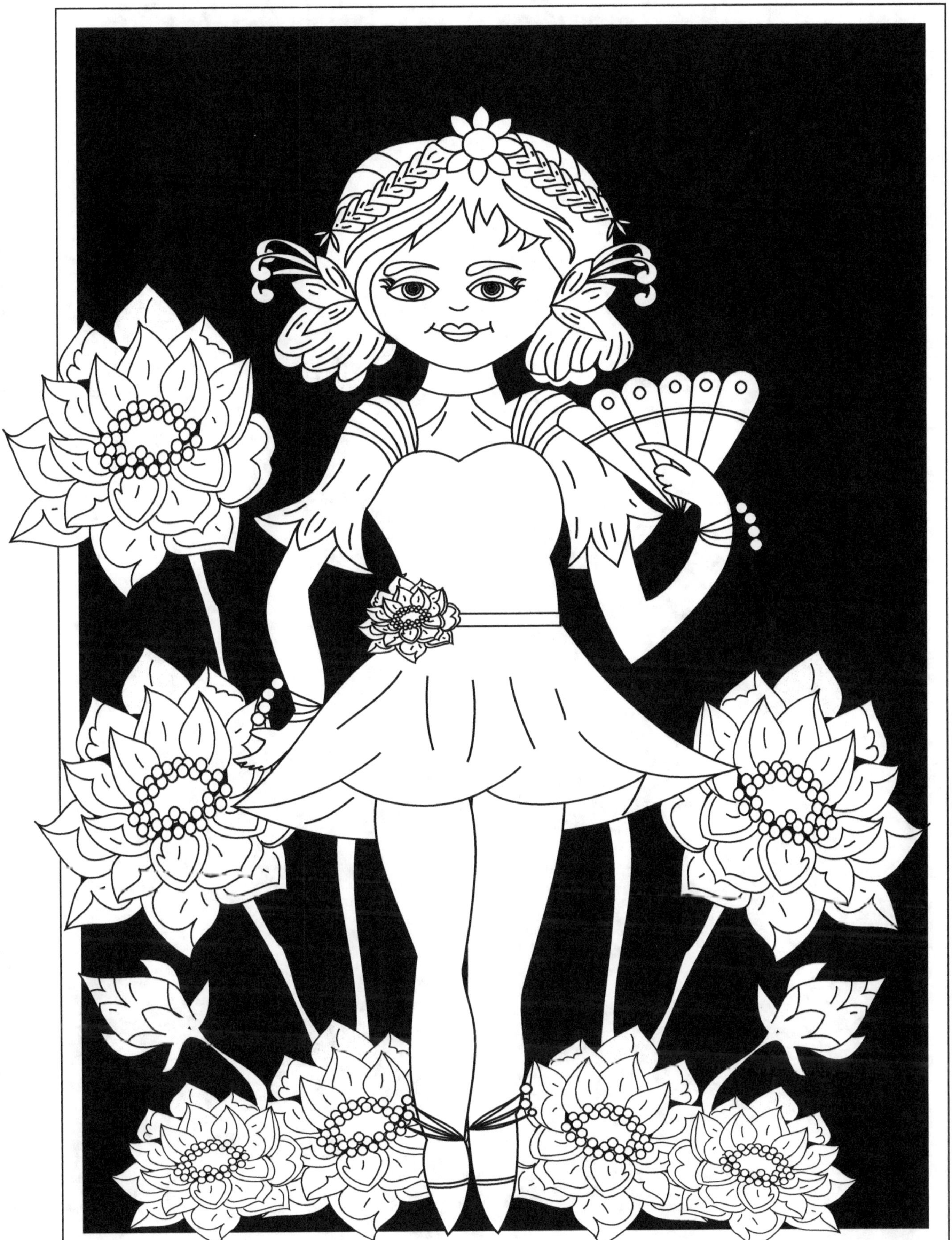

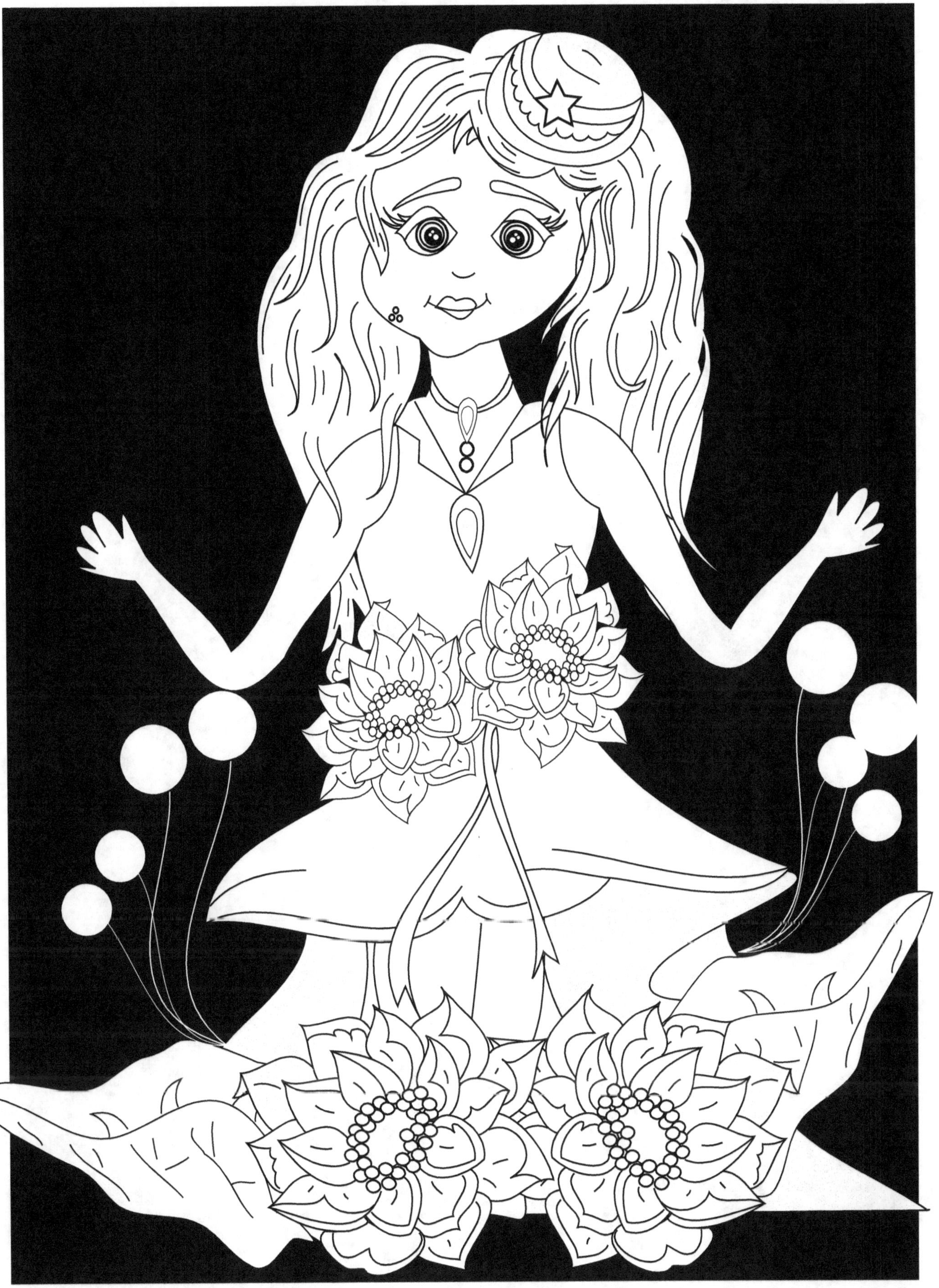

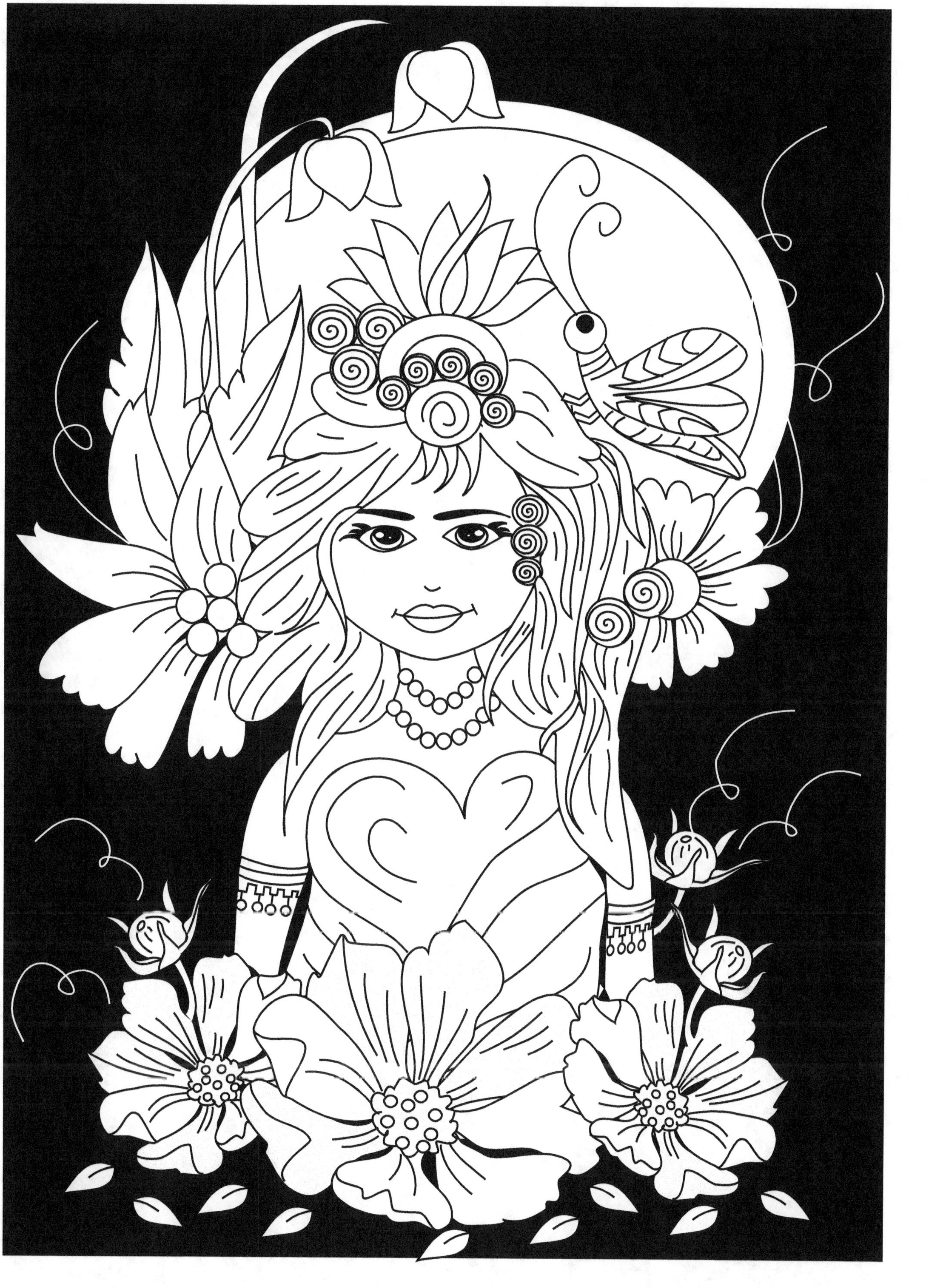

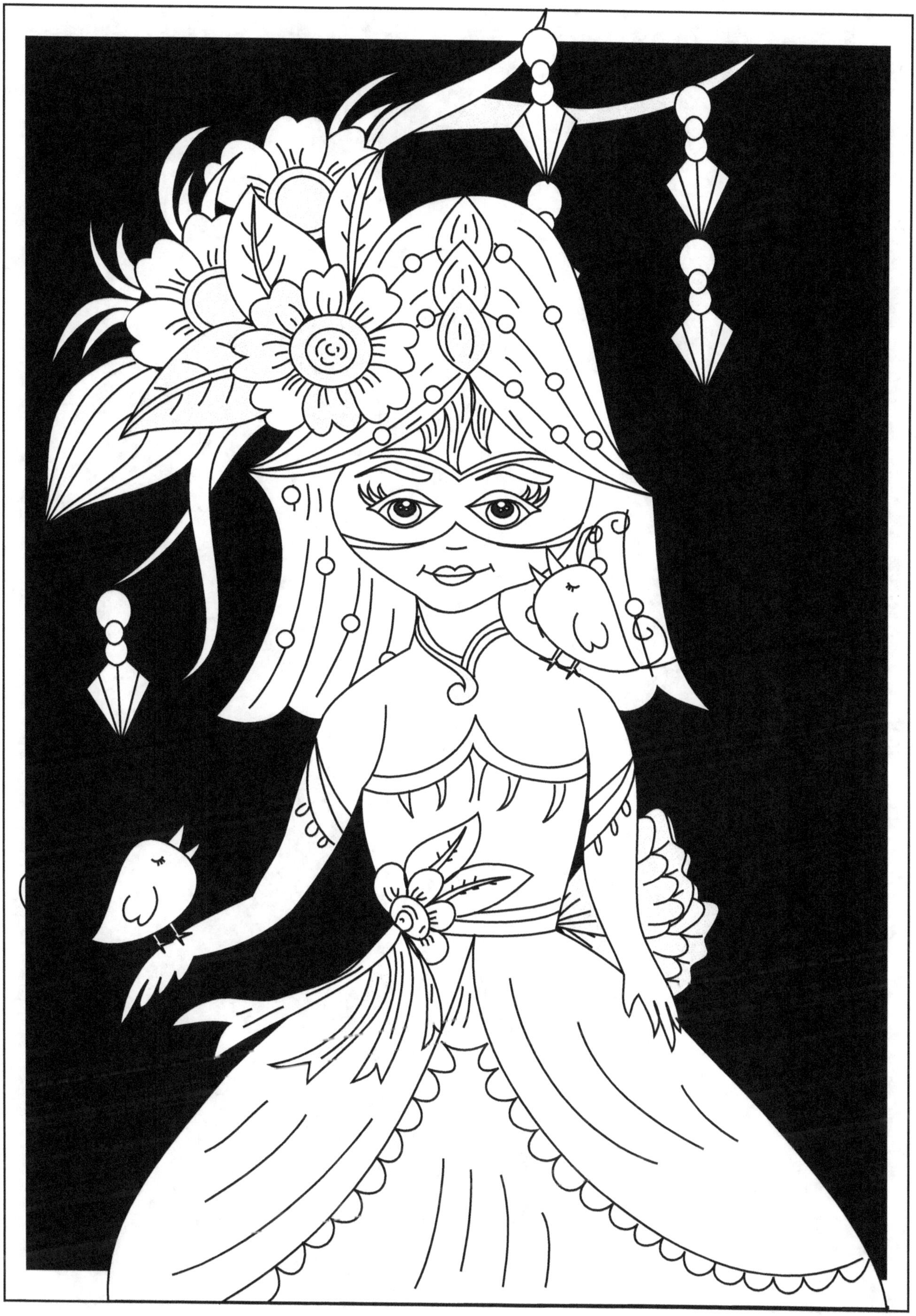

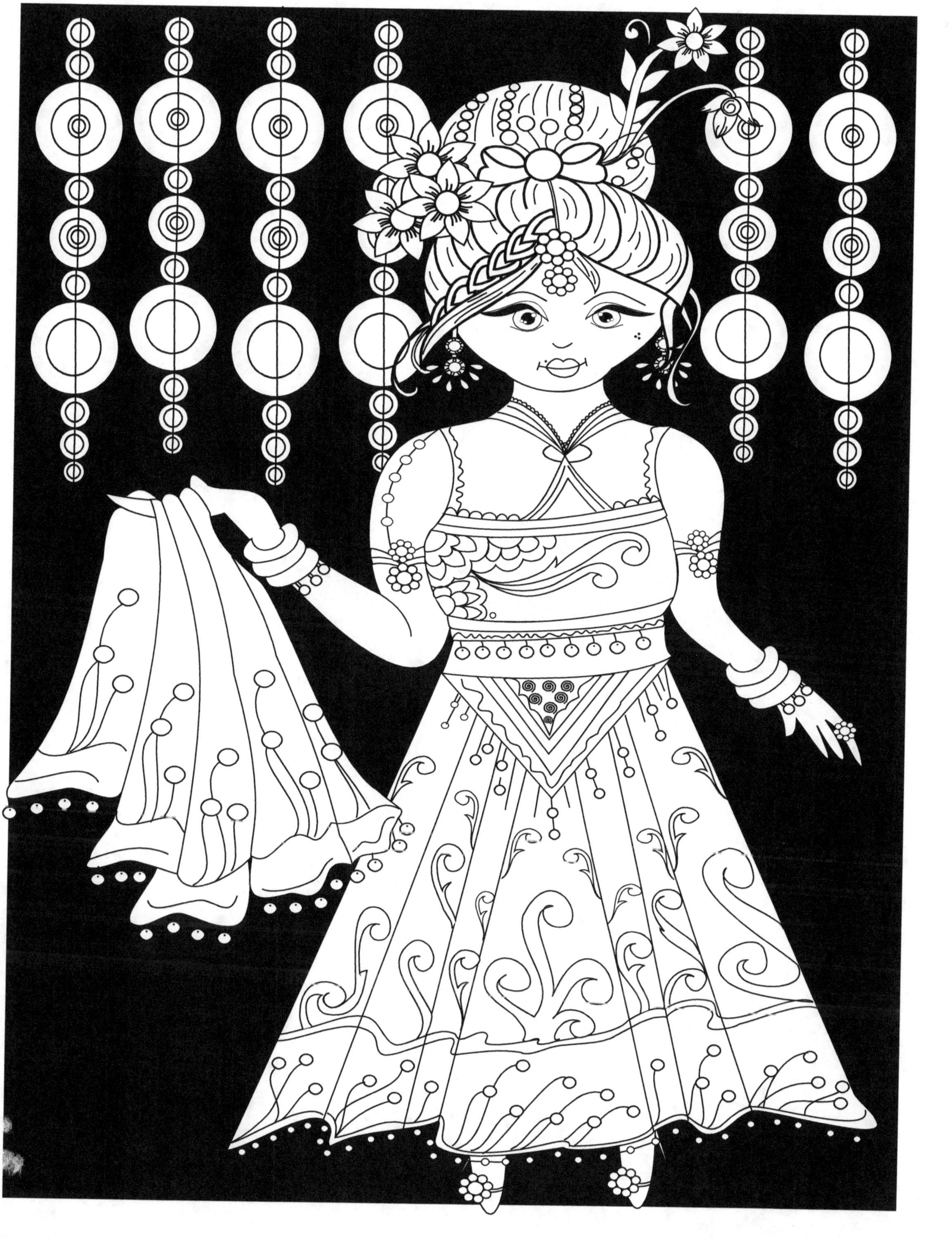

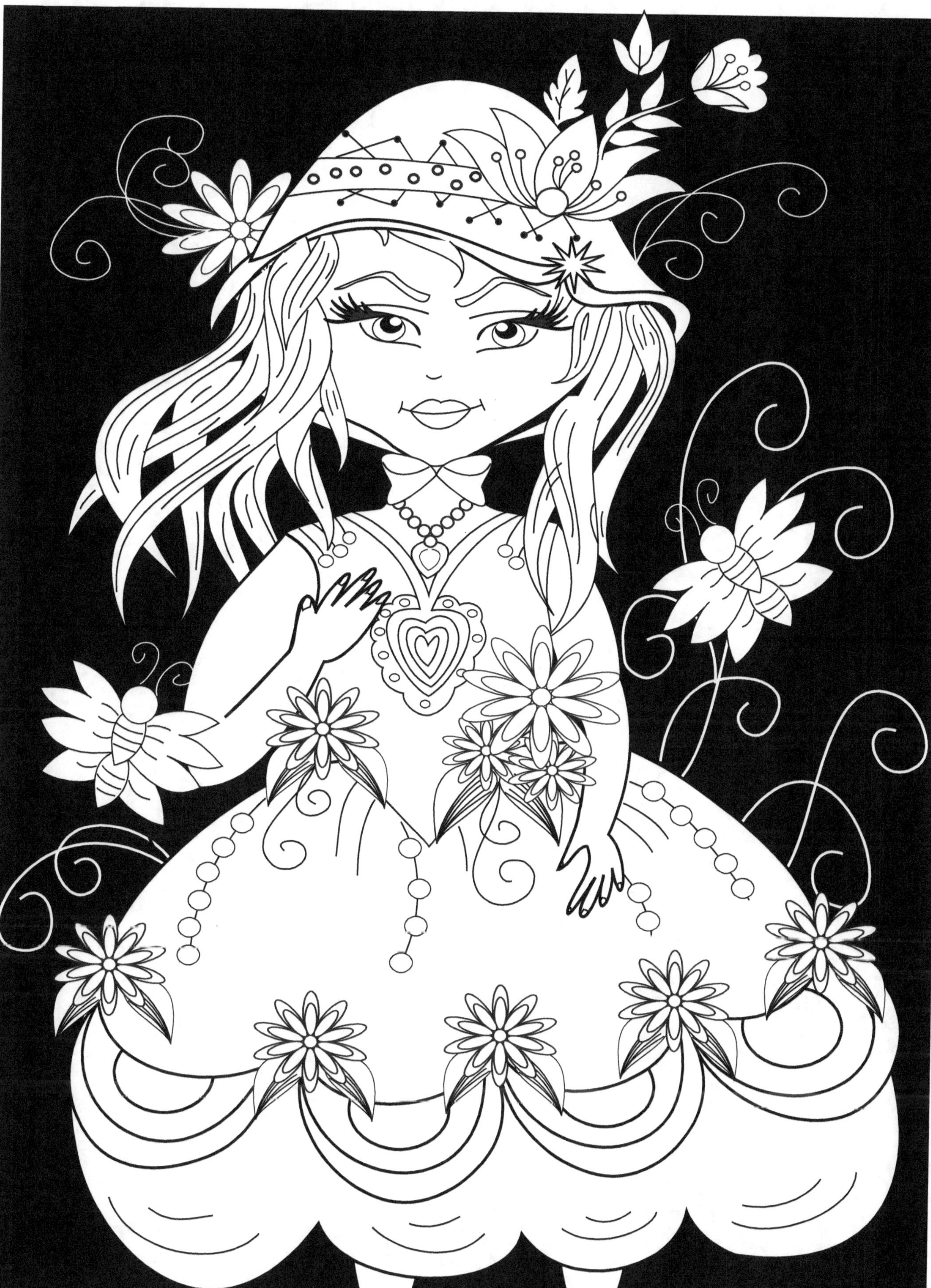

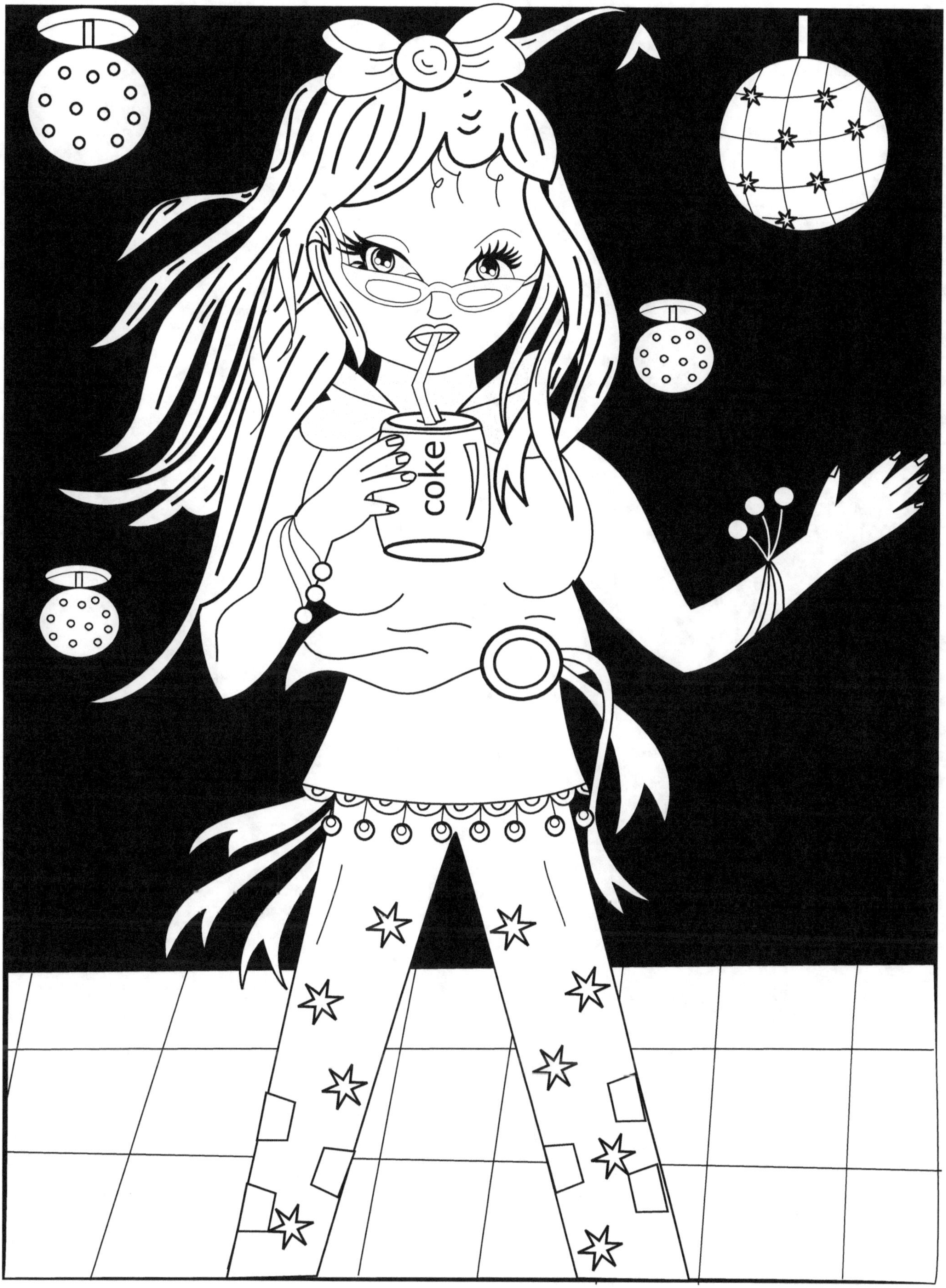
coke

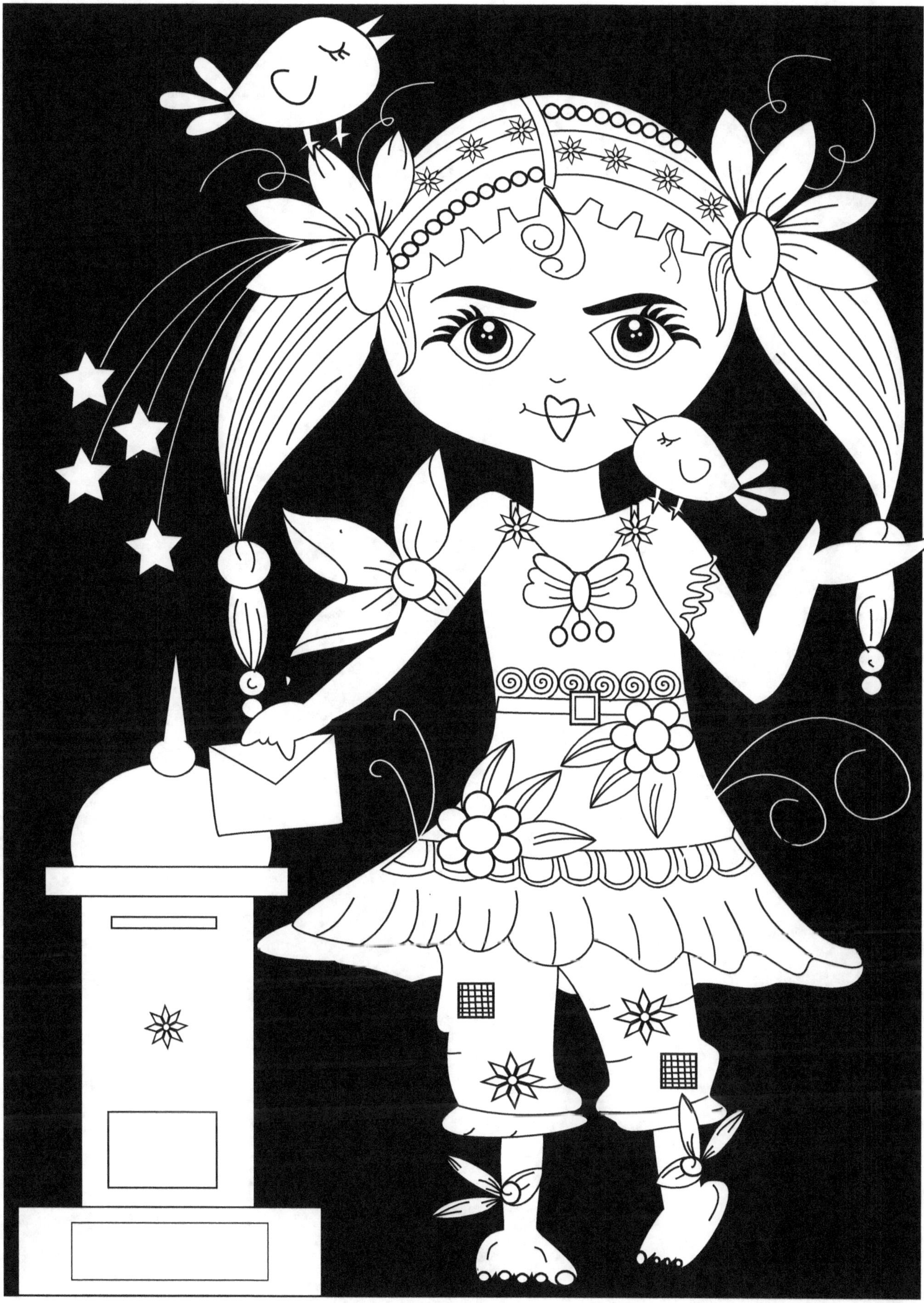

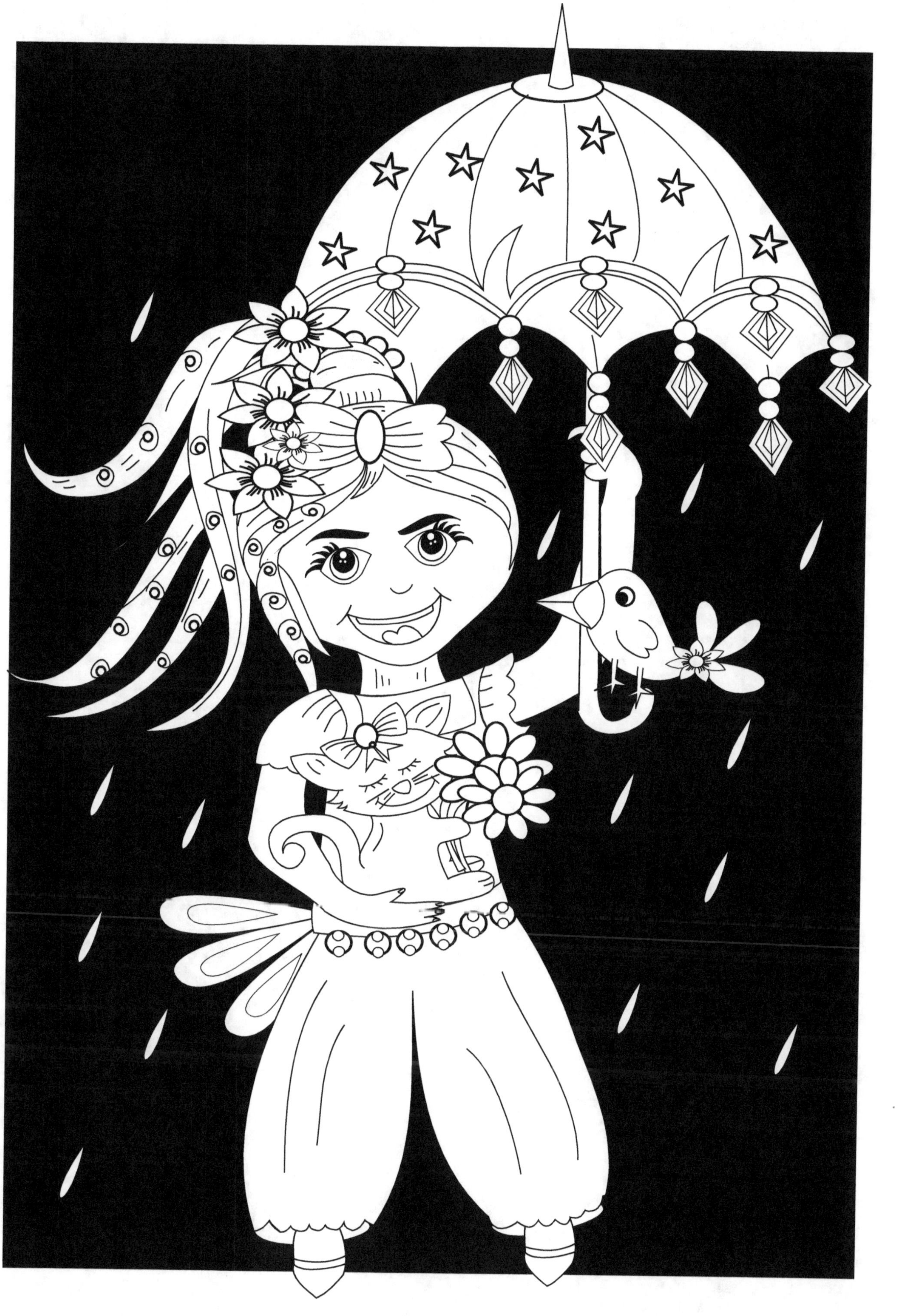

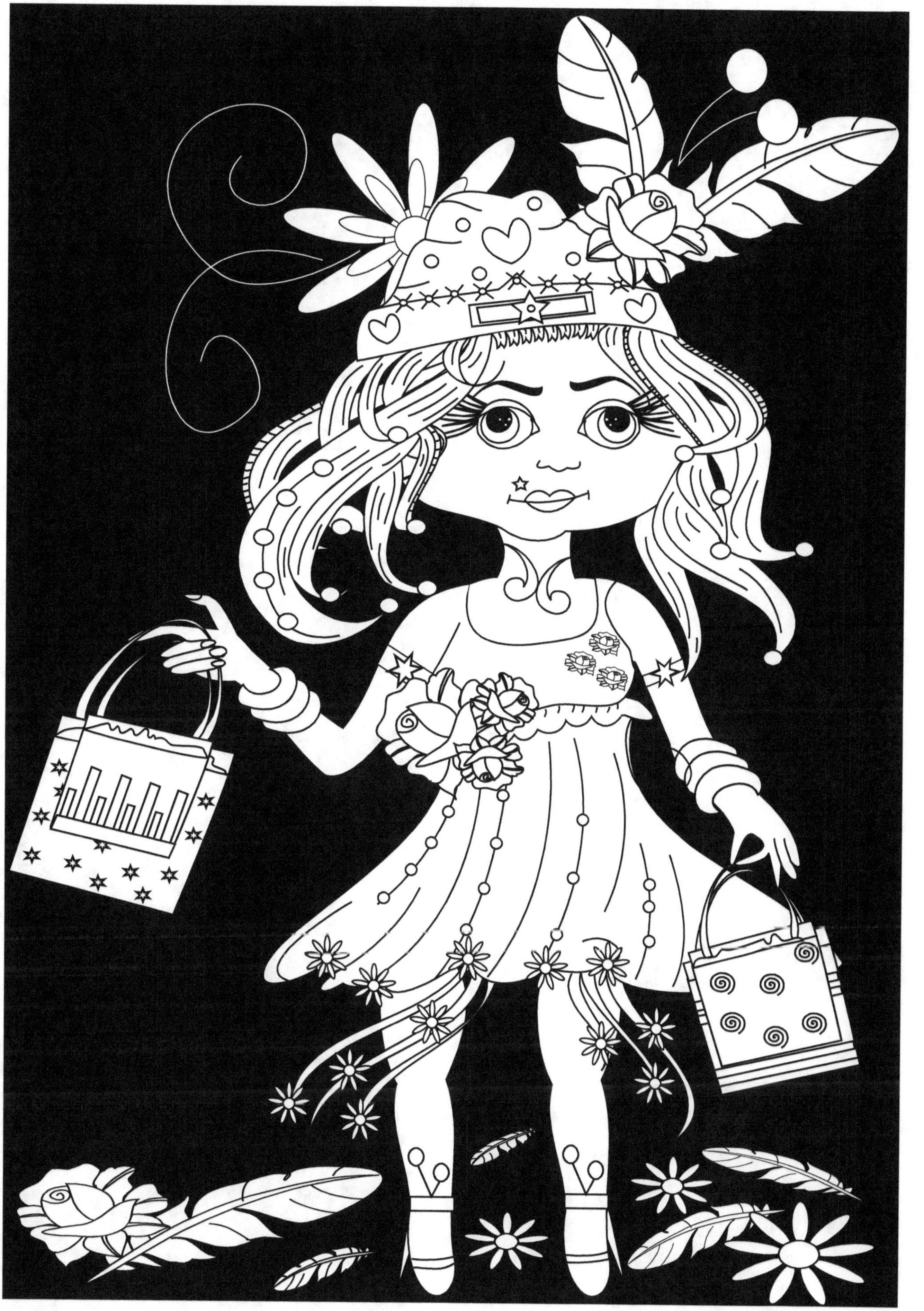

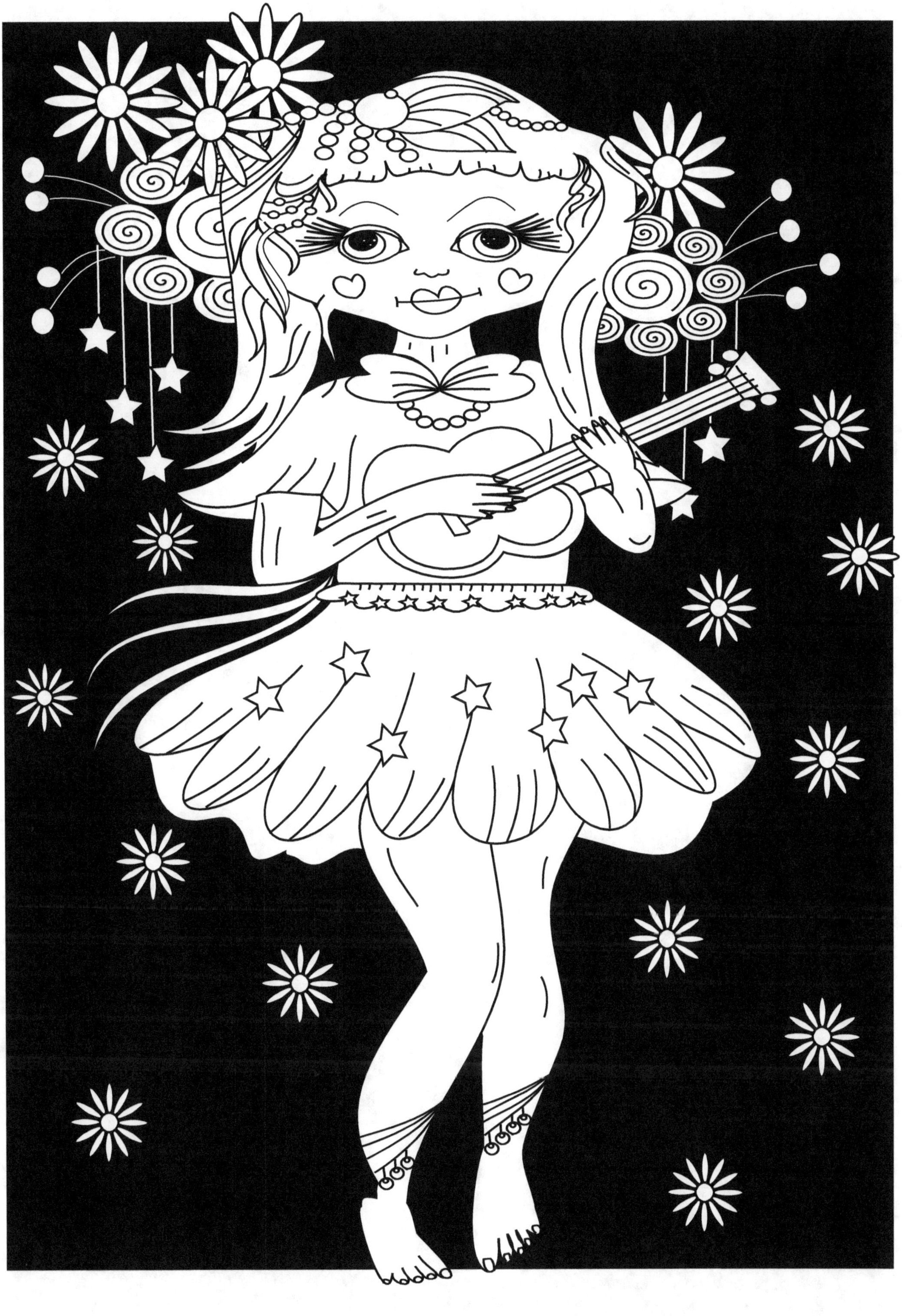

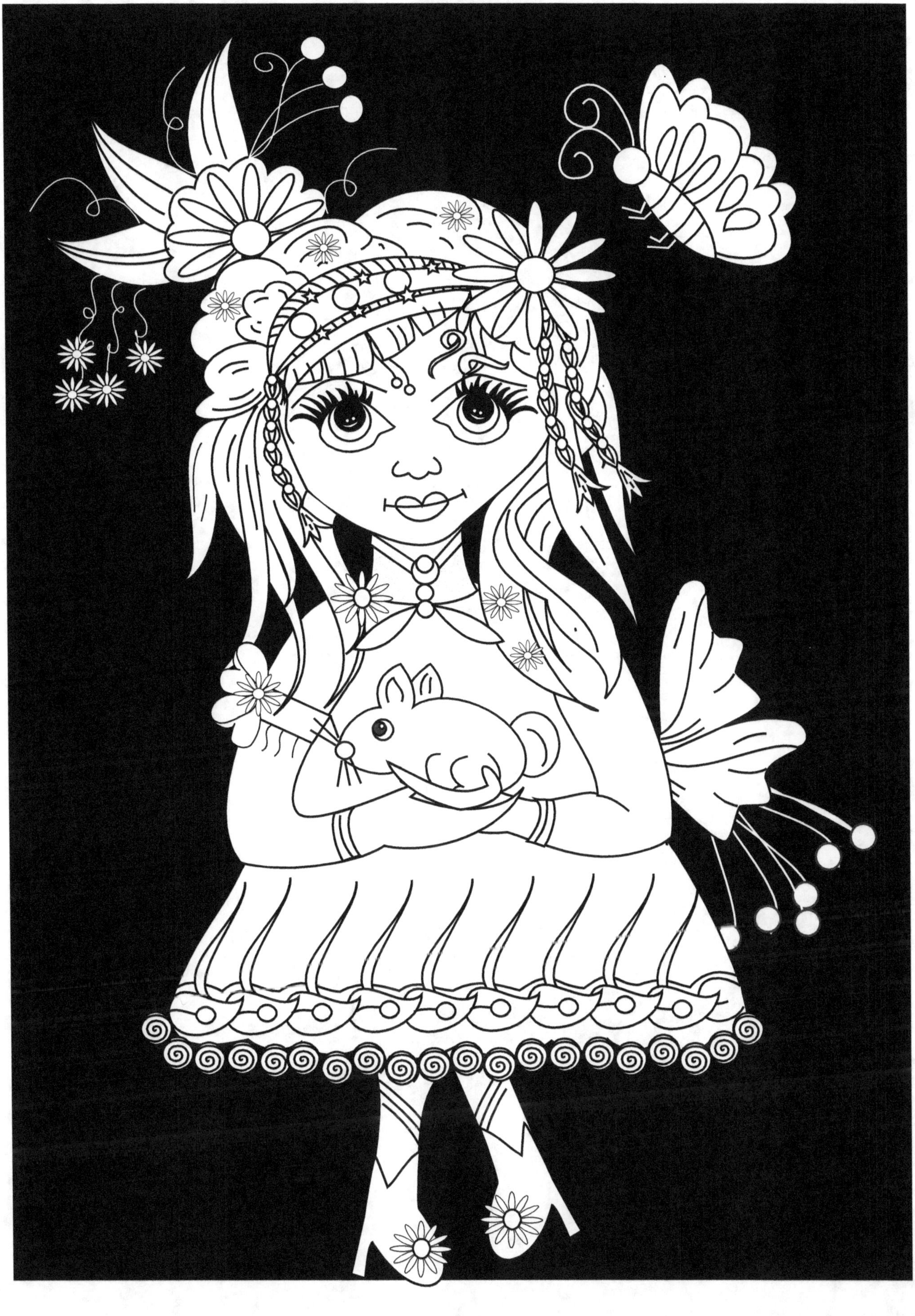

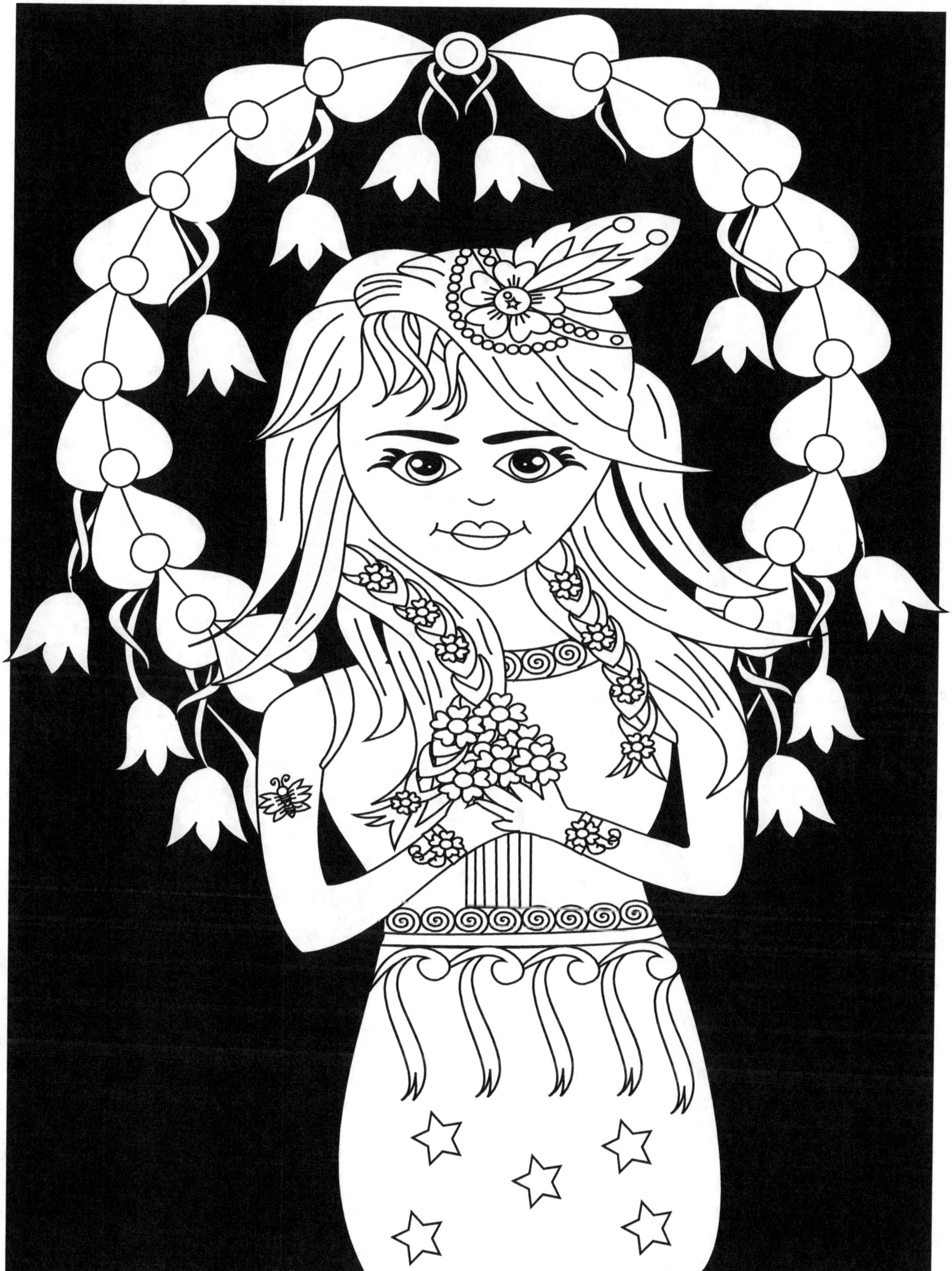

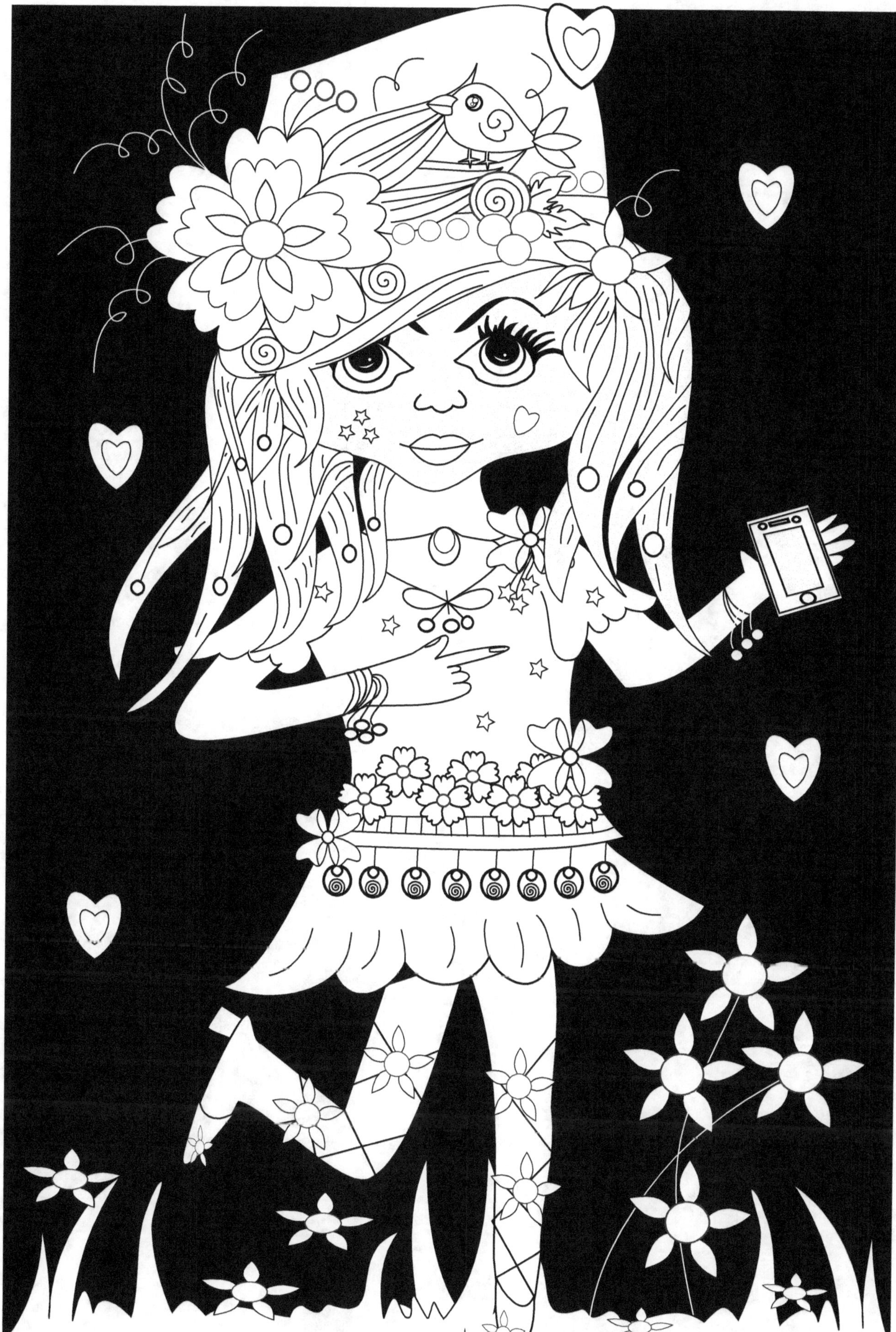

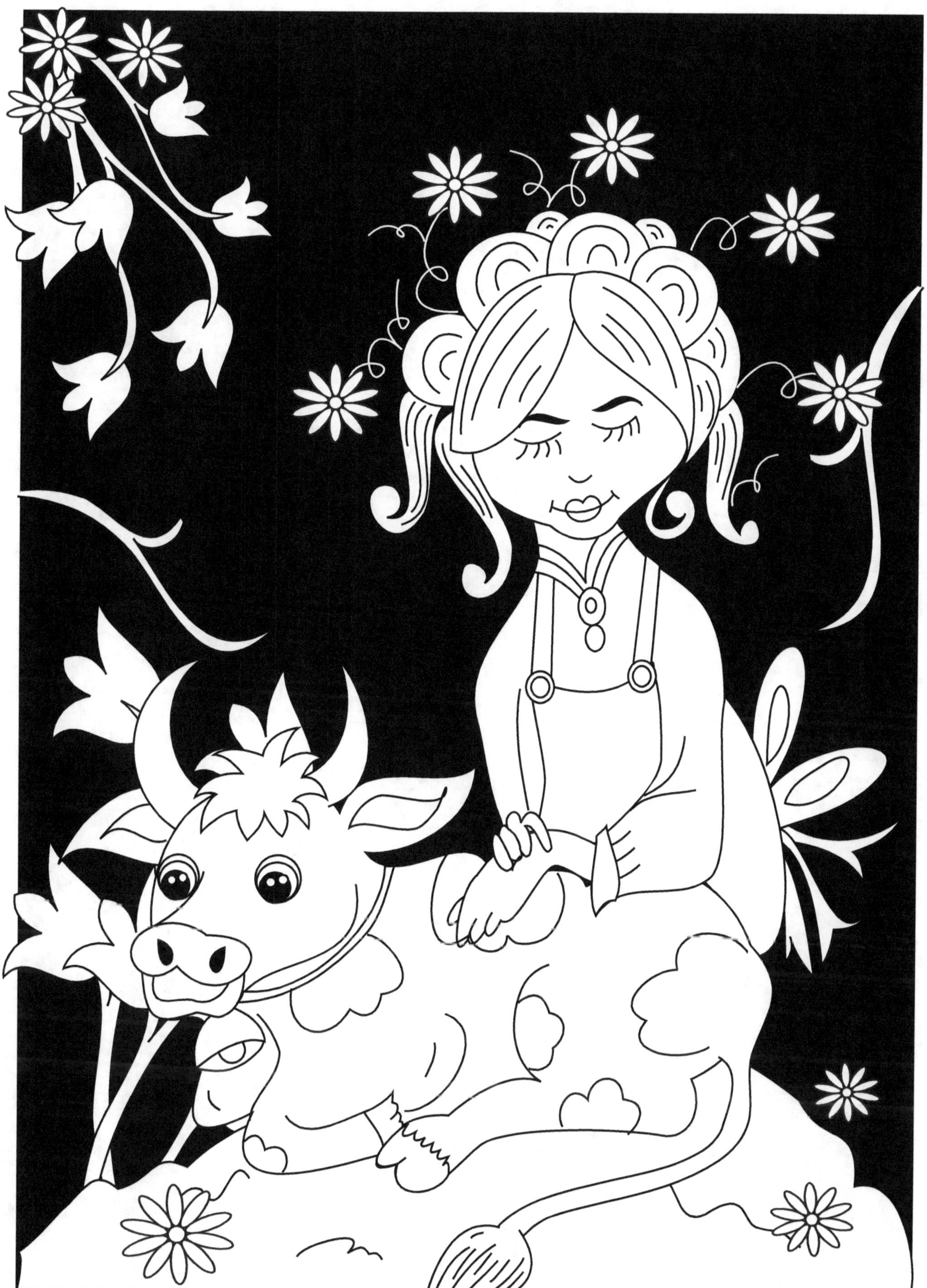

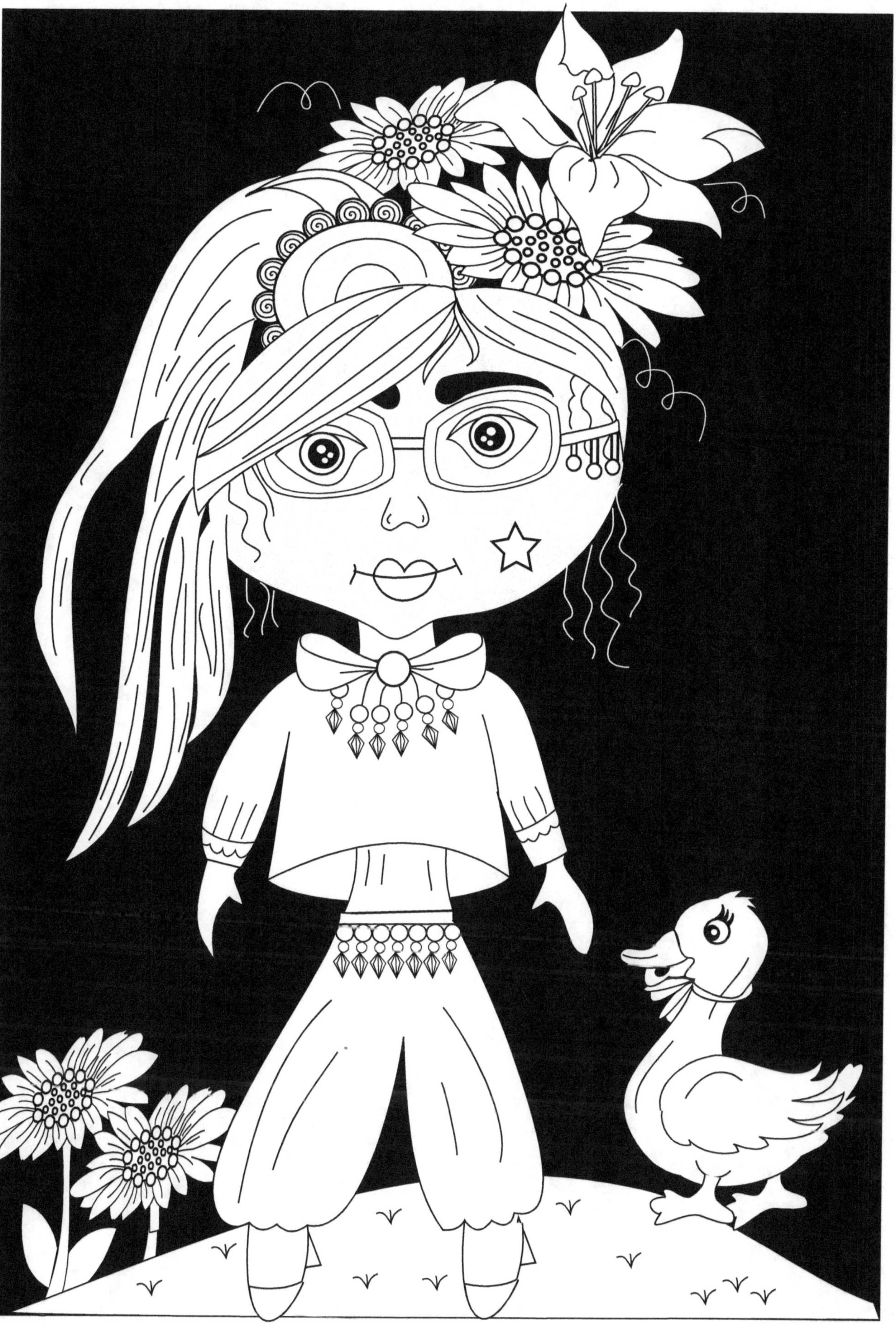

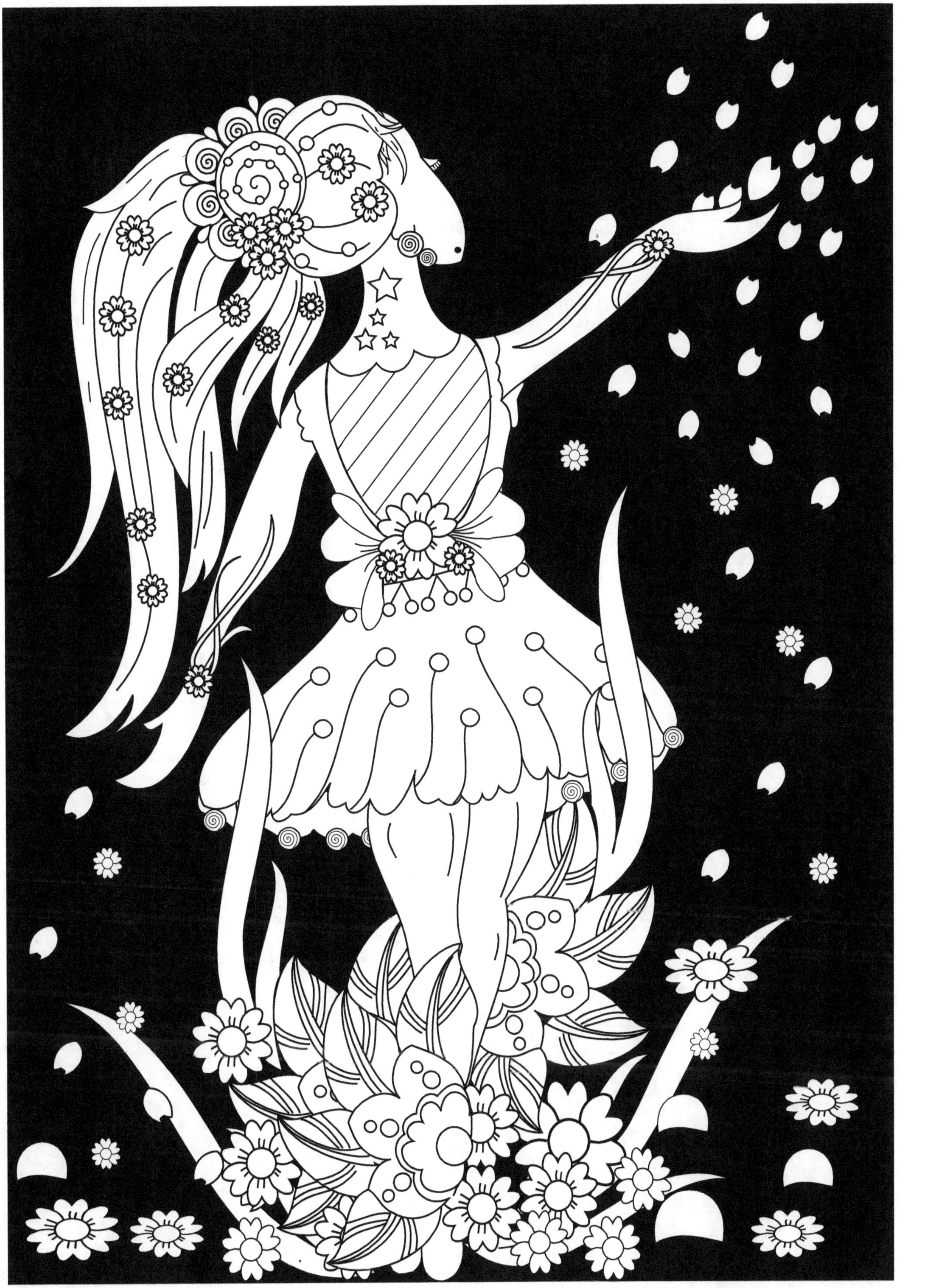

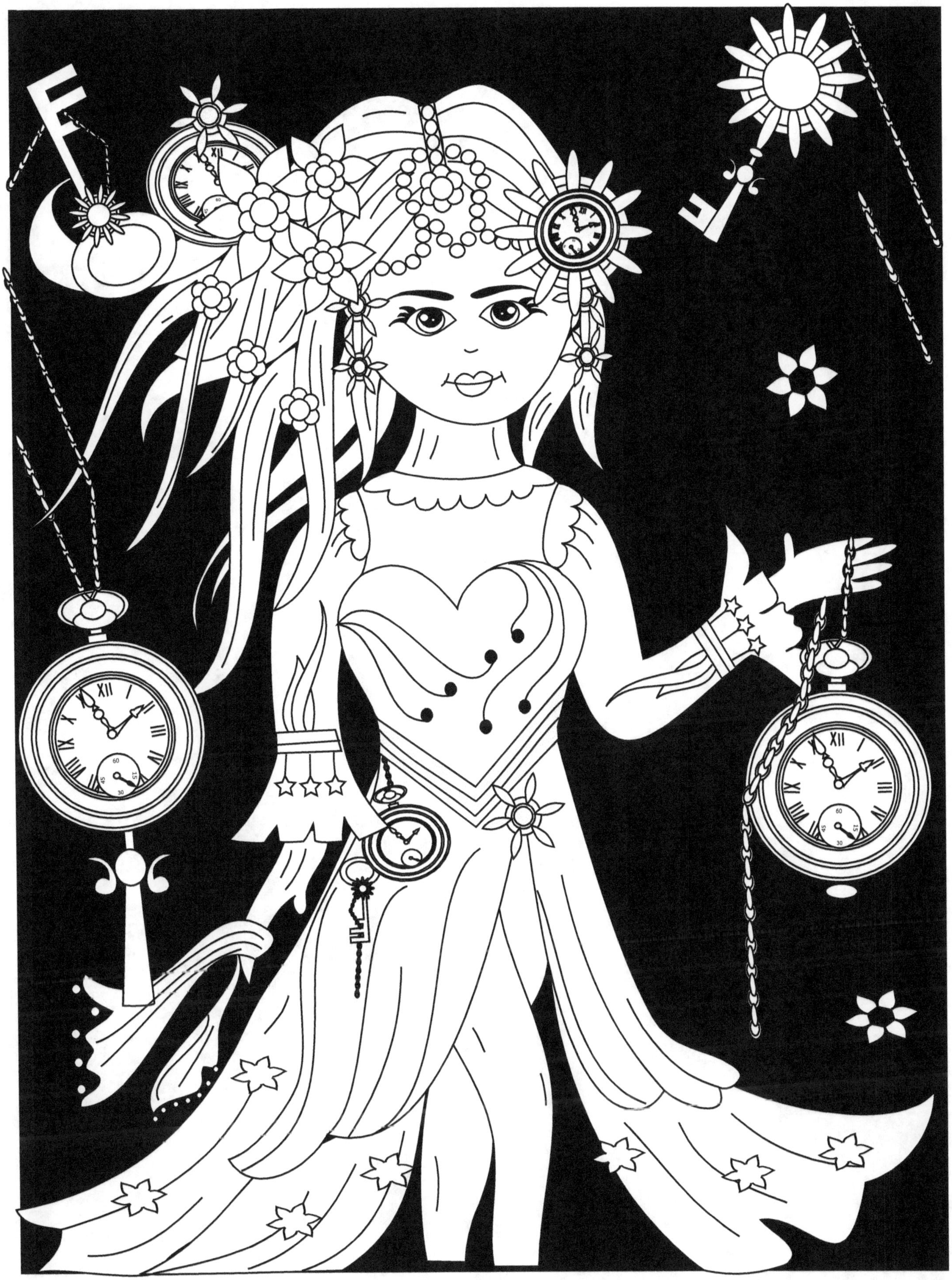

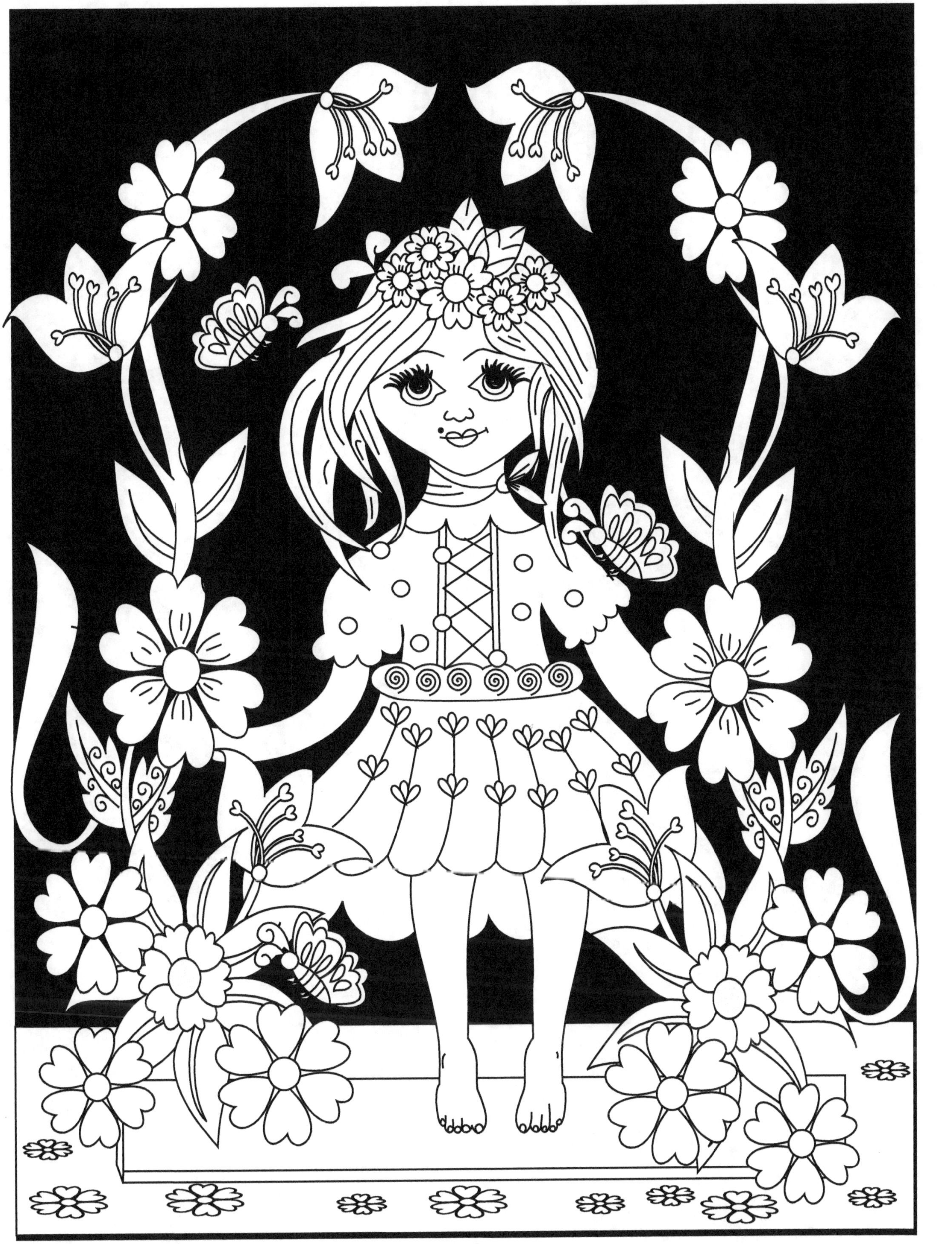

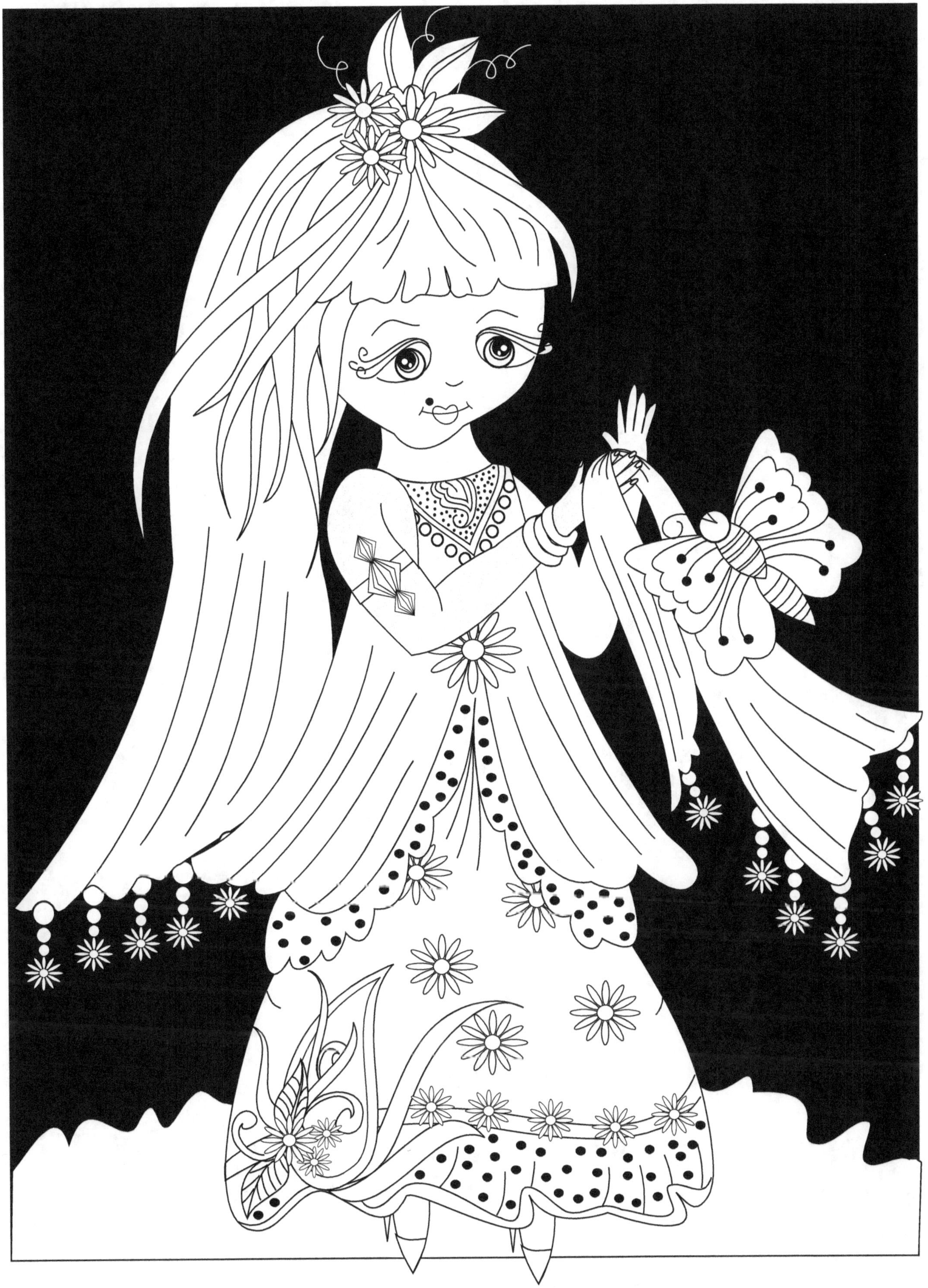

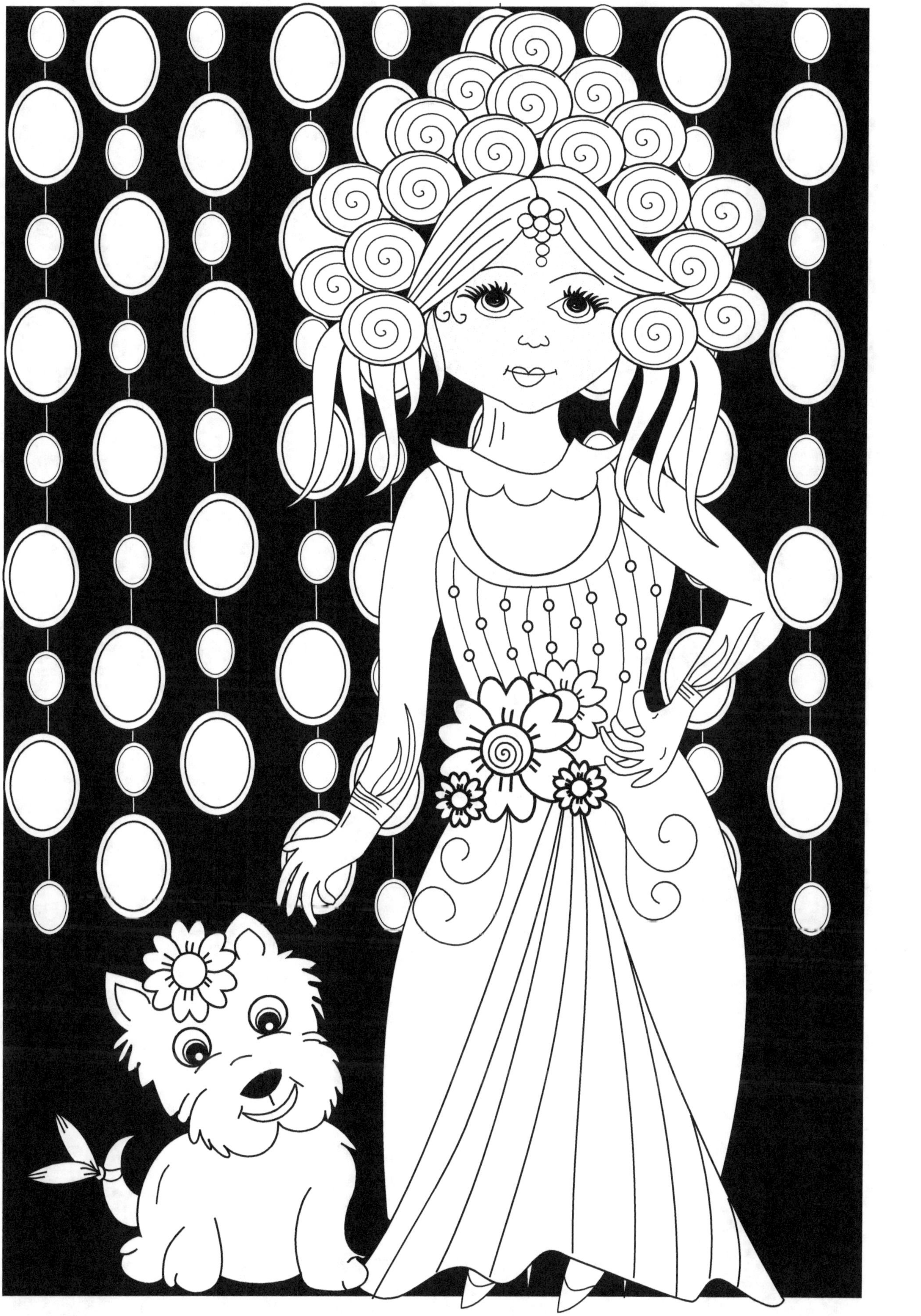

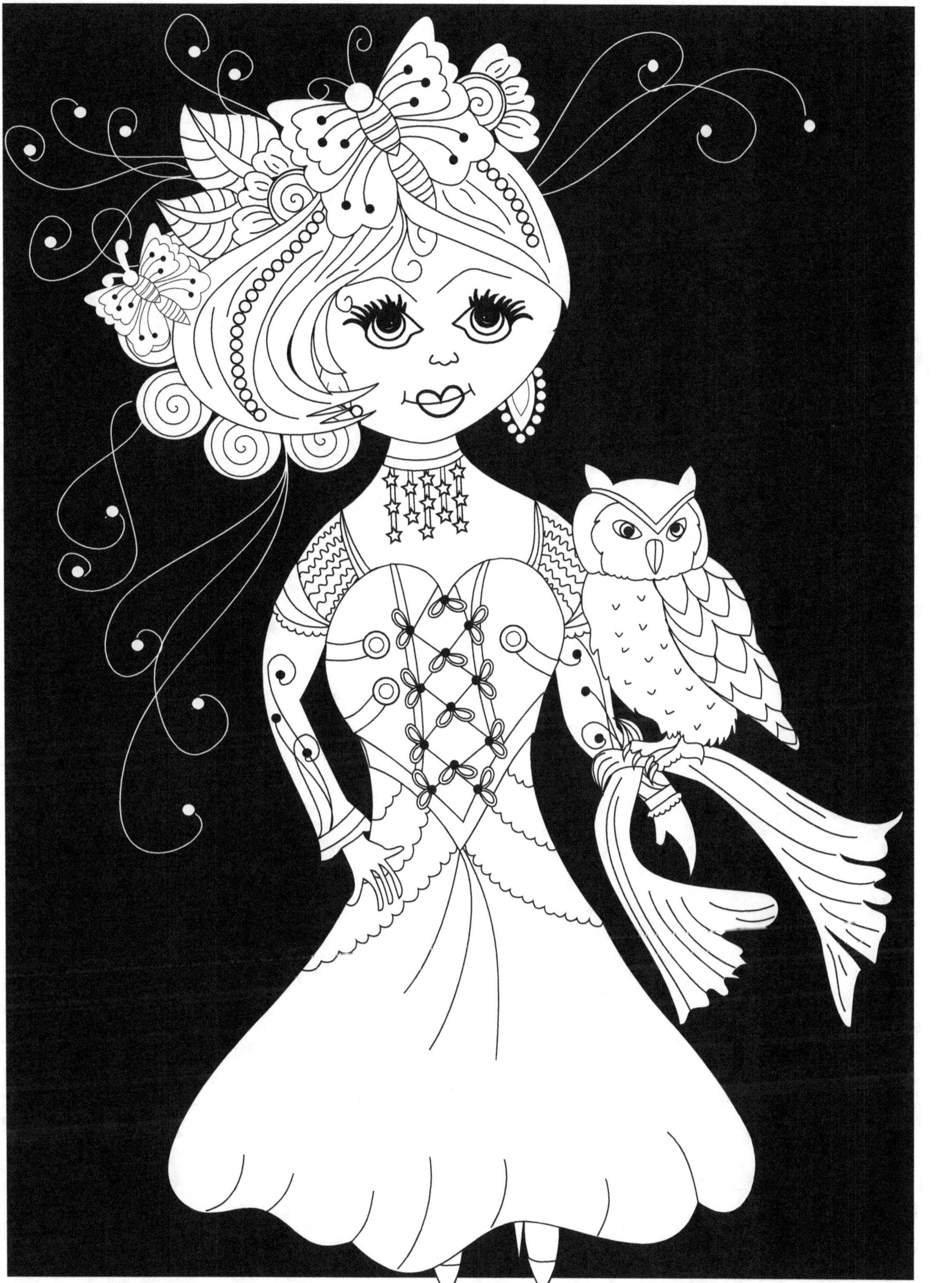

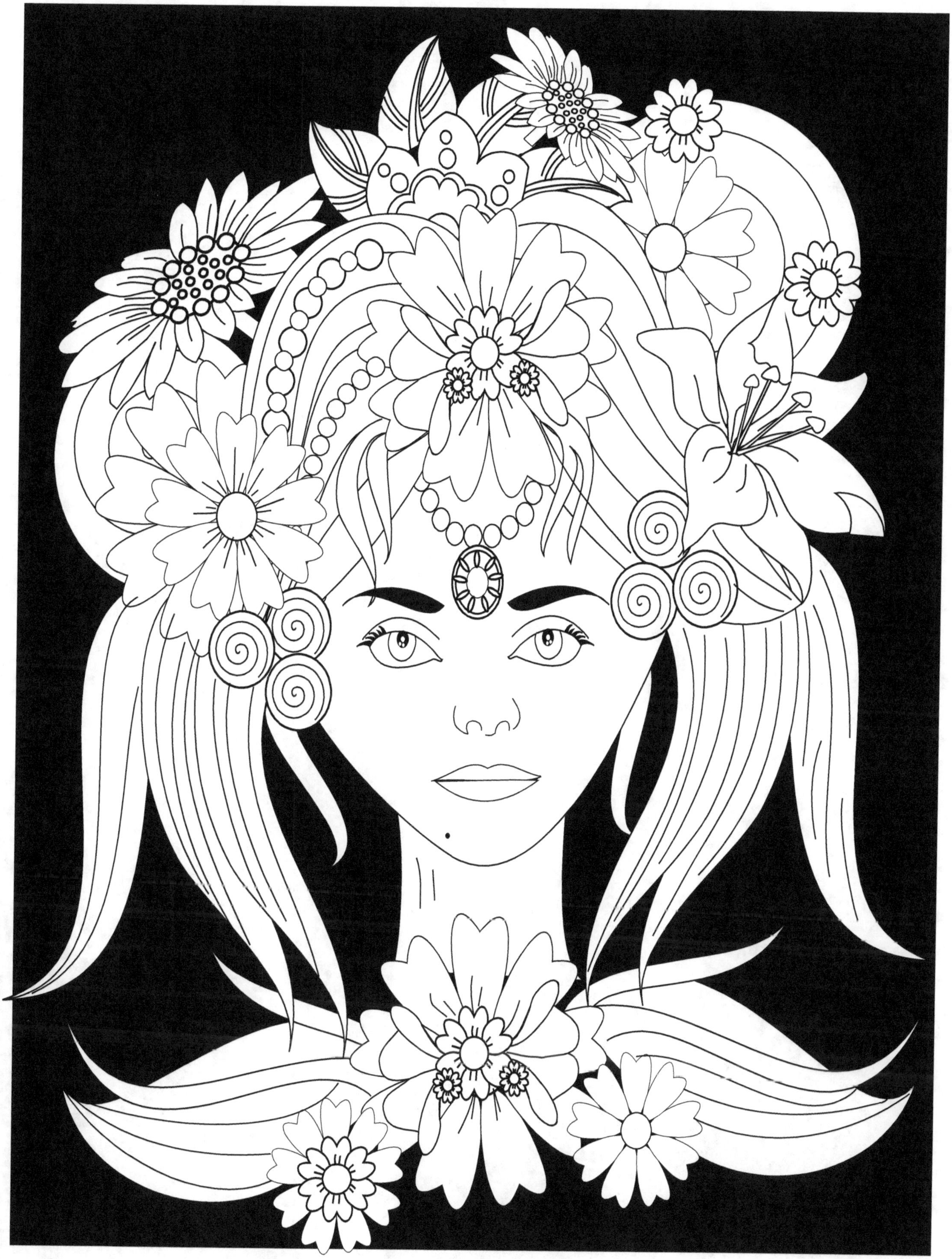

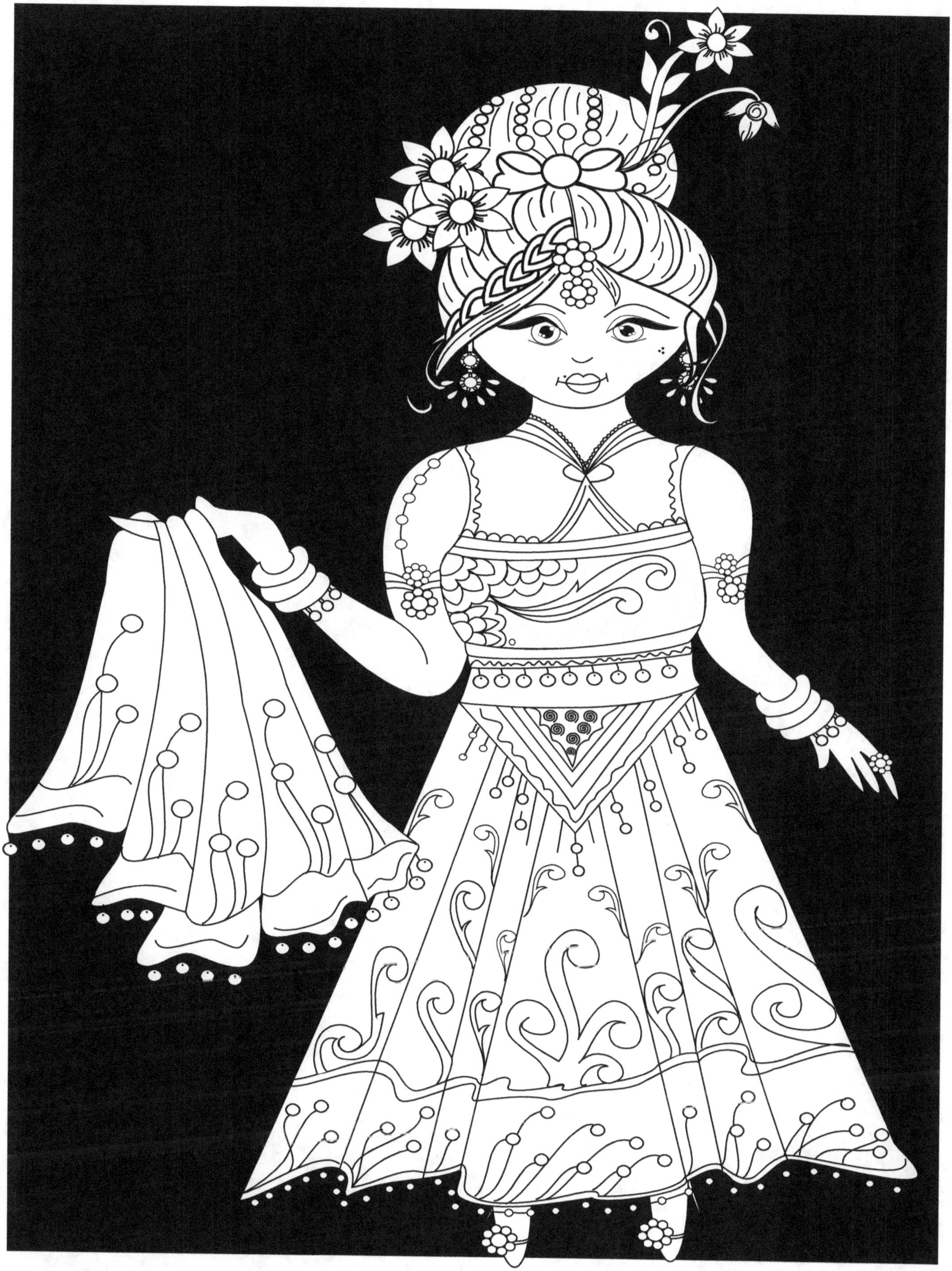

Color test

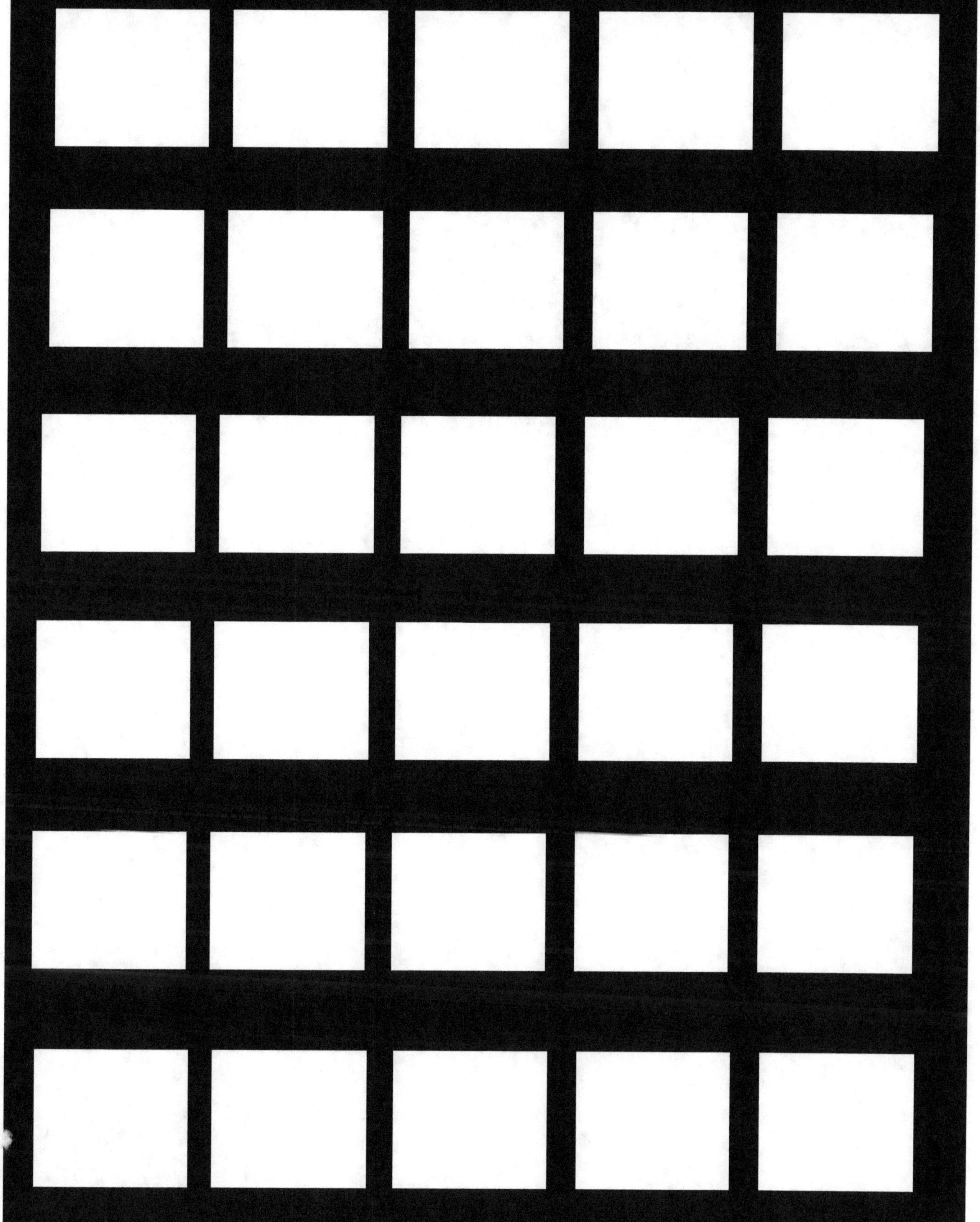

www.ingramcontent.com/pod-product-compliance
Lightning Source LLC
Chambersburg PA
CBHW080933170526
45158CB00008B/2278